MARGARET SNEAD

Cold Case True Crime Missing Persons Vol. 3

Contents

Brittanee Drexel — 1

Hang Lee — 9

Sandra Sollie — 14

Maya Millete — 26

Elizabeth Prescott — 33

Mark Himebaugh — 42

Brandon Helms — 50

Pepita Redhair — 54

Jennifer Cahill Shadle — 59

Christian Ferguson — 67

Patty Vaughan — 78

Bianca Piper — 86

Lydia Abrams — 92

Matthew Weaver Jr — 100

Christopher Kerze — 106

Eugene Martin — 110

Jayme Closs — 123

Dorothy Scott — 128

Roberta Ferguson — 136

Audrey Groat — 141

About the Author — 153

Brittanee Drexel

On a crisp autumn day, October 7th, 1991, a new life began as Brittanee entered the world, the cherished daughter of two young teenagers, Dawn and John. Despite their youth and inexperience, they embraced the daunting challenge of parenthood with determination and love. Their journey into parenting at such a tender age was fraught with challenges, testing the strength of their relationship. The pressures eventually took a toll, leading to their separation during Brittanee's early years.

Brittanee's life underwent a significant shift when her father, John, gradually faded from her daily life. However, the void left by his absence was soon filled by a new father figure. Dawn, resilient in her pursuit of happiness, found love in the arms of Chad Drexel, a dedicated military man. Their love blossomed into marriage, and Chad warmly embraced Brittanee as his own, even adopting her and gifting her his surname.

Yet, Brittanee's childhood was not without its tribulations. She faced a daunting medical challenge – persistent hypoplastic primary vitreous in her right eye. This condition cast a haze over her vision, scarring her eye and necessitating multiple surgeries. Despite their efforts, Brittanee lost her sight in that eye, a loss she faced with admirable courage.

Through these adversities, Brittanee grew into a vibrant and outgoing teenager. Her passion for soccer shone, despite her small stature. She started wearing contact lenses, a small act of defiance against her self-consciousness about her blind eye. This personal struggle ignited a spark in Brittanee, driving her towards a career in cosmetology. She aspired to uplift others, aiming to become a model to demonstrate that beauty comes in all forms.

Brittanee's life was filled with love and laughter, surrounded by a supportive family, a plethora of friends, and a caring boyfriend. However, life's unpredictability struck again as Dawn and Chad's marriage ended in divorce in 2008. This change cast a shadow over Brittanee's happiness, reflecting in her grades at school.

In a twist of fate, her biological father, John, re-entered her life, bridging the chasm of over a decade. Their reunions in Rochester were filled with small adventures – dining out, shopping sprees, and local events. John's return seemed to buoy Brittanee's spirits.

As 2009's spring ushered in warmer days, North America buzzed with the excitement of the upcoming summer. Students eagerly planned for spring break, a time of celebration and freedom. Among these students was Brittanee, who yearned to join her friends and boyfriend at a party in Myrtle Beach, South Carolina. Despite her excitement, Dawn's maternal instincts kicked in, worried about the potential for unregulated alcohol and drug use. She initially refused but softened to allow a seemingly safer alternative – a trip to a friend's house along Lake Ontario's serene beaches.

On April 22nd, 2009, Brittanee bid farewell to her mother, stepping into her friend's car. What Dawn didn't know was that this departure was the beginning of an intricate ruse. Instead of a short drive to Lake Ontario, Brittanee and her friend embarked on a clandestine 800-mile journey to Myrtle Beach. As the car vanished into the distance, Dawn was left with an unsettling premonition, unaware of the true destination and the events that would unfold.

Brittanee's journey down to Myrtle Beach was a smooth one, with the car wheels rolling seamlessly along the highway, marking her transition from the familiar streets of her hometown to the unknown thrills of a spring break adventure. Upon her arrival, Brittanee found herself amidst a group of new friends, a mix of personalities that left her feeling slightly uneasy. Sensing something amiss, she gravitated towards Peter Brushovitz, a male friend, whose company she found more comfortable.

The group's days were filled with the quintessential beach activities – volleyball games under the sun's embrace and evenings transformed into a kaleidoscope of vibrant club scenes and exuberant parties. However, by April 25th, the initial excitement began to wear thin, and tensions surfaced. A minor disagreement with the girls she was staying with left Brittanee feeling out of place, prompting her to seek refuge at the Blue Water Resort where Peter was staying.

Her solitary walk to the resort was captured by surveillance cameras along South Ocean Road. Brittanee's silhouette was seen entering the Blue Water Resort, a moment frozen in time, unaware of the significance it would later hold. The argument with her roommates, seemingly trivial at the time, escalated when one of them sent a text demanding the return of borrowed shorts. Brittanee, albeit reluctantly, set off back to her hotel at 8:45 PM, her phone busy with texts to her boyfriend, John.

Throughout the day, Brittanee and John had been in constant communication. Even as she navigated the awkwardness with her roommates, her messages to John remained casual and normal. However, suddenly, Brittanee's texts stopped. This abrupt silence was out of character, especially as she always made it a point to end conversations before stepping away. John's texts went unanswered, his calls unreturned. His growing worry escalated to the point where he threatened to inform Brittanee's mother, hoping it might provoke a response. But silence prevailed.

As hours ticked by, John's unease transformed into action. Revealing

Brittanee's secret trip to Dawn was a significant step, but he felt compelled by the unusual circumstances. Dawn, stricken with distress upon learning of her daughter's disappearance, wasted no time in contacting the authorities.

As the search for Brittanee commenced, both local police and her family scoured Myrtle Beach. They probed every possible location – bus stops, convenience stores, abandoned buildings, and natural areas. Despite their exhaustive efforts, no trace of Brittanee emerged. The only clue lay in the mysterious pings from her phone: first at Surfside Beach, then at Georgetown, each time moving further south, before the digital trail went cold.

The investigation intensified, with police searching the homes of known sex offenders in both Myrtle Beach and Georgetown, and examining a hotel room in Georgetown County linked to a person of interest. Raymond Moody was identified as a potential lead, but no concrete evidence emerged.

As days turned to weeks, and weeks to months, and then years, the mystery of Brittanee's disappearance deepened. Her family, refusing to give up hope, launched widespread awareness campaigns, set up hotlines, offered rewards, and displayed billboards – anything to keep the search alive. Dawn, fueled by a mother's unyielding love, made regular trips to Myrtle Beach, distributing flyers and keeping Brittanee's story in the public eye. Deep down, she feared the worst but remained determined to find closure.

Seven years into the relentless search, with little progress and fading leads, Dawn made a drastic decision. She moved to South Carolina, dedicating her life to finding her daughter. Then, in June 2016, a glimmer of hope appeared – a new lead, unexpected and potentially significant, emerged, reigniting the search for Brittanee.

The case took a perplexing turn with the emergence of a lead from Taqwan Brown, an inmate at McCormick Correctional Institution. Serving time for an unrelated manslaughter charge, Taqwan's revelation cast a new shadow over the decade-long search for Brittanee. He narrated a harrowing tale implicating Timothy DeShawn Taylor, another inmate convicted for robbery, in the alleged sexual assault and murder of Brittanee, along with the involvement of approximately ten other men.

Taqwan's account, delivered from behind bars, described a chilling scene. He recounted that, while still a free man, he had ventured to a stash house in McClellanville to deliver money to Timothy's father. This small town hauntingly aligned with the last known location of Brittanee's phone signal. It was in this house, Taqwan claimed, that he witnessed the brutal assault on Brittanee. In a desperate bid for freedom, Brittanee purportedly burst through the front door, only to be violently recaptured by Timothy and dragged back inside. The story took an even darker turn when Taqwan recounted hearing two gunshots shortly afterward.

The skepticism around Taqwan's story was inevitable. Why would an inmate come forward with such a tale after seven long years, without any apparent coercion or benefit? His credibility waned further when, three years later, his story morphed yet again, claiming he saw Brittanee alive on two additional occasions beyond the day he initially stated she was murdered. With no corroborating witnesses or evidence to support Taqwan's claims, his narrative stood precariously on shaky ground.

Amidst this mire of allegations and denials, Timothy DeShawn Taylor vehemently refuted any involvement in Brittanee's disappearance. His consistent denial, combined with corroborating alibis from friends and family for the day Brittanee vanished, cast further doubt on Taqwan's account.

Thus, what initially seemed like a breakthrough in the case dissolved into a red herring, diverting police resources and hope. This turn of events also positioned Taqwan unfavorably within the prison system, as his role as an informant earned him the unwelcome title of a snitch.

By 2019, the case once again froze in the cold grip of uncertainty. A decade had passed since Brittanee's disappearance in 2009. Ten years of torment for her loved ones, filled with sleepless nights, agonizing over whether they would ever see Brittanee again. A decade of speculation, hope, and despair, wondering if she was still alive, or if not, how and where her life might have tragically ended.

In May of 2022, the cold case of Brittanee Drexel unexpectedly burst back into the spotlight, a resurgence powered by a confession that upended years of speculation and dead ends. This pivotal confession came from Raymond Moody, a name that would soon become infamous in connection with Brittanee's disappearance.

To understand the gravity of this breakthrough, one must delve into the complex tapestry of Raymond's life. His early years were marred by a tumultuous family life, where he was raised amidst the chaos of an alcoholic mother and a violent father. Such an environment deprived him of the chance to thrive in a nurturing and stable home. As he stepped into adulthood, Raymond sought to distance himself from his troubled past, moving to California and joining the military in a quest for a new beginning.

However, Raymond's narrative took a sinister turn. Despite being a family man with three children, he was harboring dark secrets. Known to law enforcement across various states, Raymond's criminal record was alarming. In 1983, he was convicted as a sex offender for assaulting children, but served only half of his 42-year sentence. Released on parole in 2004, his criminal behavior persisted, leading to further arrests in 2008 for indecent exposure and in 2010 for failing to register as a sex offender.

During the period of Brittanee's disappearance, Raymond was not confined behind bars. He was among the individuals scrutinized when police investigated local sex offenders in Myrtle Beach and Georgetown, including a search of Raymond's property. However, the lack of direct evidence initially cleared him as a suspect.

Thirteen years later, the investigation refocused on Raymond Moody. A renewed probe into local sex offenders and a shift in the narrative led to growing suspicions about his involvement in Brittanee's case. Charged with obstruction of justice, Raymond was detained for questioning. Facing the intensifying scrutiny of law enforcement, Raymond finally shattered the long-standing silence with a confession, admitting to the murder of Brittanee Drexel.

According to Raymond's account, he forcefully kidnapped Brittanee while she was returning to her hotel, a crime unseen by witnesses or cameras. He then transported her to a remote location, where he committed the unthinkable – he assaulted and strangled her. The following day, he disposed of her body in the woodlands near his property in Georgetown, an area not far from where Brittanee's phone had last signaled.

Acting on Raymond's confession, law enforcement officers embarked on a grim search, which led them to unearth the tragic remnants of Brittanee - a skull and several bones, buried four feet underground. Forensic experts, through the analysis of dental records, confirmed the heartbreaking truth - the remains were indeed Brittanee's.

The revelation of Brittanee's fate and the identity of her killer reopened past traumas for Raymond's other victims. Among them was Carrie Harding, whose encounter with Raymond when she was just eight years old is a testament to her bravery and resilience. Carrie's narrow escape from Raymond's clutches, thanks to her quick thinking and a memorable green bumper sticker on his vehicle, later played a critical role in his identification and subsequent legal battles.

Raymond, with his crimes against Brittanee and others, was sentenced to a 42-year prison term. However, the justice system saw him serve only half of this sentence, a detail that left a bitter taste for those who sought complete justice for his numerous heinous acts.

The long and tortuous journey to uncovering the truth about Brittanee Drexel's disappearance and the subsequent confession of Raymond Moody opened old wounds, but also brought a measure of closure to a case that had lingered in uncertainty for far too long.

Hang Lee

On the 12th of January in 1993, a 17-year-old named Hang Lee departed from her family's residence in St. Paul, Minnesota to attend a job interview. It was a chilly, dim evening in the Midwestern city, which had just experienced its initial significant snowfall of the winter. This evening marked the onset of a tragic series of events.

Hang Lee was born on October 9th, 1975, in a refugee camp in Laos, a small country in Southeast Asia. Her family belonged to the Hmong ethnic group. During the 1960s and '70s, amidst the United States' involvement in Southeast Asia, the Hmong were often collaborators with the American forces against the North Vietnamese and Pathet Lao.

Following the downfall of the Hmong forces, backed by the United States, in Laos's internal conflict known as the secret war, many Hmong faced harsh persecution from the Laotian government. Consequently, numerous Hmong individuals sought refuge in camps within Laos and in neighboring Thailand. Hang Lee's parents were among these refugees. Shortly after her birth, her family relocated to the United States and settled in St. Paul, Minnesota, a common destination for many Hmong families. Living as refugees, Hang's family faced financial hardships, and her parents had limited English proficiency. They resided in public housing in St. Paul's North End area.

By January 1993, Hang had become a successful student at Highland Park High

School, with aspirations to attend the University of Minnesota the following year. She was a talented storyteller, eager to share the Hmong experience in the United States through her writing. Described by her family and coworkers as reserved, kind-hearted, and a bit gullible, Hang was known to be easily swayed by practical jokes.

To support her family financially, Hang worked part-time at Wong Cafe, a Chinese restaurant, where she served as a cashier and dishwasher. Seeking better-paying opportunities, she inquired about other jobs from friends. One of her friends, Kia Lee (no direct relation), who was employed as a receptionist at a painting and carpentry business on St. Paul's East Side, informed Hang about a job opening there. Eager for the chance, Hang agreed to meet Kia's employer, despite later police reports suggesting that Hang had some reservations about Kia's intentions.

Before leaving for her interview on that fateful January night, Hang spoke to her younger brother, 15-year-old Koua, cautioning him, "If I don't come back, come and look for me."

In spite of her apprehensions, Hang left her home. She was last seen dressed in a black leather jacket, black pants, and a t-shirt featuring the heavy metal band Skid Row, her long black hair styled in a fashion typical of the early '90s.

Hang's premonitions tragically proved accurate. After her interview, she didn't return home, and there were no signs of her in the following days. Realizing something was amiss, her parents, hindered by language barriers, struggled to report her missing. Initially, police considered her a potential teenage runaway, but evidence in her room suggested a more alarming scenario. Hang had been saving for college and left all her money at home on the night she vanished. Her absence at Wong Cafe, where she missed shifts and didn't collect her paycheck, was out of character. She also left behind her purse, which contained self-defense items, indicating that if she had run away, it was unlikely she would leave these essentials.

Her brother Koua expressed concerns about Nikki Lee, Hang's friend, leading the police to question Nikki. In police interviews, Nikki's accounts were contradictory. Initially, she claimed Hang didn't go to the interview and left with unfamiliar men, supporting the runaway theory. However, months later, Nikki altered her story. She confessed to fabricating the earlier account, partly out of hope and partly due to her boss's alleged instructions, fearing his retaliation.

Nikki hoped Hang had simply left and would return. But Hang's situation involved Mark Steven Wallace, Nikki's boss, who had asked if she knew someone needing a job, leading to Hang's recommendation. Nikki found this odd, as Wallace's business seldom had customers or work. Additionally, she was uneasy about young boys visiting Wallace's office and his talks of modeling opportunities, including photographing her for a supposed friend, though nothing came of it.

Changing her story, Nikki told police that after Hang's interview, Wallace offered them a ride. They transferred from his truck to a Chevy Cavalier. After dropping Nikki off at her home in Frogtown, St. Paul, Hang, now in the front seat, was last seen with Wallace. Nikki ceased cooperating with police and media after hiring a lawyer. Meanwhile, Wallace emerged as a significant suspect in Hang's disappearance.

Months into the St. Paul police's investigation of Hang Lee's disappearance, they uncovered that Mark Steven Wallace had prior convictions for two sexual assaults in Washington County. These assaults, committed in 1987, included one against a 16-year-old girl whom Wallace had lured with a job offer. He was said to have kidnapped and assaulted her, threatening her life and her family's if she spoke out. Wallace was eventually apprehended by an undercover officer whom he approached similarly. Convicted in 1988, he served approximately three years before being released on supervised release, which ended just a week before Hang's disappearance.

When questioned about Hang, Wallace confirmed interviewing her and claimed he dropped her off near her workplace, aligning with Nikki's account. However, he then ceased cooperation with the police, hiring a lawyer. Despite ongoing investigations, Hang's case grew cold until a significant lead emerged in 2009.

In 2009, Wallace's Maplewood home was foreclosed, allowing the police to search the property with cadaver dogs. The dogs showed interest in the garage, suggesting the possibility of human remains under the concrete floor. Despite drilling for better detection, only one dog indicated the presence of remains, insufficient for a full excavation, leading the police to halt their investigation there.

A new development occurred in 2016, 23 years after Hang's disappearance. Wallace fled a traffic stop near Andover and was later found at a motel in Woodbury with a 20-year-old woman. She revealed that Wallace was her friend's father and had offered her accommodation in exchange for housework. Initially amicable, this arrangement eventually deteriorated. Wallace was arrested after attempting to escape from the motel room.

In a harrowing twist to Mark Steven Wallace's already troubled history, a police complaint filed by a woman in 2016 painted a grim picture of his actions. The woman, who had previously filed a no-contact order against Wallace, alleged that he subjected her to physical and verbal abuse. This encounter wasn't isolated to just verbal altercations; when police located her in a motel room, she displayed clear signs of physical assault – exhibiting bruises and signs of malnutrition, but no accusations of sexual assault were made against Wallace at this time.

This incident led to Wallace's arrest and subsequent charges, including felony kidnapping intended to cause great bodily harm and felony stalking, alongside a misdemeanor for drug possession. While the latter charges were eventually dropped, Wallace was convicted and sentenced to 54 months in prison for the kidnapping charge. This event, occurring years after Hang Lee's disappearance, which had faded from public consciousness, suddenly thrust her case back into the limelight.

What reignited interest in Hang Lee's case were the chilling revelations from the kidnapping survivor during Wallace's trial. She informed the police of her awareness regarding Hang Lee's disappearance and Wallace's connection to it. She alleged that she had confronted Wallace about Hang Lee, to which police records indicate Wallace ominously remarked that Hang had entered his business but "never came out." The complaint also detailed the survivor's claim that Wallace had threatened her similarly, boasting about his ability to eradicate blood evidence and his expertise in dismembering bodies.

This alarming information was shared with the St. Paul Police Department by authorities in Washington County, where Wallace faced trial and conviction. While the St. Paul police did not publicly comment on these developments or Wallace's conviction, Hang Lee's case remained an active and open investigation.

In a subsequent legal development in August 2019, after serving his prison sentence, Wallace was committed to a treatment program by an Anoka County court, based on his 2016 kidnapping conviction, his 1988 assault convictions, and psychiatric evaluations labeling him as a dangerous individual with psychopathic tendencies. Wallace attempted to appeal this commitment in September 2020, but the court reaffirmed its decision, citing his history of convictions as justification. He remains a patient in the treatment center.

Despite these developments, Mark Steven Wallace has never been formally designated as a suspect in Hang Lee's disappearance. He remains a person of interest, a shadowy figure in a case that continues to intrigue and alarm those who follow it, leaving a lingering question about what really happened to Hang Lee.

Sandra Sollie

Sandra Sollie, affectionately known as Sandy, entered the world on December 10, 1955, the cherished youngest child of Dominic and Nancy. She blossomed in the small, close-knit community of Oakfield in Genesee County, New York. With four older siblings to look up to, Sandy's childhood was filled with laughter and love. Known for her effervescent personality, she became a beacon of joy and kindness in her community.

From a young age, Sandy formed a deep and lasting friendship with Tina Fredo, who would later reminisce about Sandy's exceptional qualities. Tina fondly remembered Sandy as someone whose heart knew no bounds, someone who embraced life with open arms and offered unconditional love and support to everyone she met.

Sandy's educational journey began at Oakfield-Alabama Central School, where she was a diligent student, though her vivacious nature often led to gentle reminders to focus more on her studies and less on socializing. Nonetheless, her infectious personality left a lasting impression on both her peers and educators.

As Sandy transitioned into adulthood, her dreams and aspirations began to take shape. She envisioned a future filled with the joys of motherhood, a dream she shared closely with her sister Donna. The sisters shared a bond that went beyond siblinghood; they were confidantes, sharing everything from school experiences to teenage musings about boys.

Sandy's path led her to Ralph Sollie Jr., and with him, she hoped to turn her dreams of family life into reality. However, the tides of life had other plans. The early years of their marriage saw them part ways, with Ralph eventually remarrying a woman who was once Sandy's hairstylist. The aftermath of their divorce brought its share of challenges and tensions, particularly around the arrangements made during their separation.

By the spring of 1994, Sandy was embracing a life of independence, living in an upstairs apartment of a duplex off Route 350. Here, she created a cozy home for herself and her beloved charcoal poodle, Jessie. Although an accident at her workplace, Eastman Kodak Company, had left her on disability due to a head injury, Sandy found solace in her serene domestic life.

The silver lining during this challenging period was the joyful news of her pregnancy. By May 1994, Sandy was in the advanced stages of her pregnancy, eagerly anticipating the arrival of her son, whom she had already lovingly named Brandon Michael. Her transformation during this period was remarkable; those close to her noticed a renewed sense of purpose and joy as she prepared for motherhood.

Sandy's nurturing spirit was evident in her meticulous preparation for Brandon's arrival. She transformed a room in her apartment into a nursery, filled with all the necessities and comforts for her son. Regular prenatal visits became a part of her routine, as she devoted herself to ensuring a healthy pregnancy.

The community shared in Sandy's excitement, with plans for a baby shower taking shape. Set for June 12th, it was an event that symbolized hope and new beginnings. However, fate had other plans, as Sandy mysteriously vanished more than two weeks before the shower, leaving behind unanswered questions and a community in distress.

The last known activities of Sandy's day paint a picture of a woman diligently attending to her daily errands. From picking up a prescription in Newark to dropping off clothes at a second-hand shop, her day was typical of a soon-to-be mother preparing for the arrival of her child. She was also seen assisting Ed Miller, an elderly friend, with his errands - a testament to her kind-hearted nature.

However, the interactions with her ex-husband Ralph on that day add a layer of complexity to her story. While Ralph recalled a mundane exchange about a car issue, others suggested there might have been more to their interaction. As the details of her disappearance began to unfold, the interactions between Sandy and Ralph, particularly on her last known day, drew increasing scrutiny from investigators and those close to her.

It was not unusual for her to spend days, sometimes even a week, without reaching out to her close circle of friends and family. This tendency of hers meant that initially, her absence didn't raise any immediate alarms among those who knew her. The community, accustomed to her independent nature, assumed she was in contact with someone else, even if they hadn't heard from her personally.

Meanwhile, a distressing incident occurred in nearby Rochester on the same day Sandy was last seen. Four-year-old Kaylee Poulton disappeared, sparking a massive search operation. Kaylee's case quickly dominated the headlines, drawing significant attention and resources from local and federal agencies. The sense of urgency in finding Kaylee was palpable, with everyone in the vicinity considered a potential suspect due to the proximity of the abduction.

While the search for Kaylee intensified, Sandy's absence quietly slipped under the radar. It wasn't until June 2nd, a notable time after her last sighting, that Jay Whiting, Sandy's landlord for five years, felt something was amiss. Whiting's concern stemmed from Sandy's uncharacteristic delay in rent payment and her unresponsiveness to both calls and visits. The mystery deepened for Chief John Ellis, who upon inspecting Sandy's residence, found nothing overtly amiss. The apartment was orderly, her car was parked as usual, but Sandy, her purse, and her beloved poodle Jessie were nowhere to be seen.

Three days later, the concern escalated when both Sandy's neighbor and family members contacted the police about her unexplained absence. This prompted the Macedon Police, in collaboration with state authorities, to officially begin an investigation into Sandy's disappearance. A thorough examination of her apartment yielded little evidence of foul play. Yet, one peculiar detail stood out - her keys were found inside her locked apartment and car, suggesting she had left willingly but intended to return.

The focus of the investigation was on her routine activities, particularly her habit of walking her dog along the Erie Canal, just a short distance from her apartment. The search teams scoured the area, extending their efforts to the dense forests beyond the canal. Helicopters buzzed overhead, while teams on foot and ATVs combed through the terrain and divers explored the canal. Despite their exhaustive efforts, no trace of Sandy was found.

As the search expanded across Wayne County and into Rochester, the investigation delved deeper into Sandy's personal connections. Police meticulously went through her address book, contacting each person listed and investigating any messages left on her answering machine during her absence. Despite their thorough approach, senior investigator William Bowling confessed that the case was perplexing, with no concrete evidence to explain Sandy's disappearance. However, the situation took a suspicious turn when a review of Sandy's financial records revealed anomalous activities.

In the days following her disappearance, Sandy's credit card was used 14 times, amounting to transactions that seemed unlikely to have been made by Sandy herself. Charges at a men's clothing store, and purchases of beer and cigarettes, raised eyebrows. Notably, the transactions ceased after May, adding to the mystery.

The investigation intensified as police contacted stores where the card was used, hoping to gather descriptions or surveillance footage of the individuals involved. The break in the case seemed imminent when surveillance tapes from two stores revealed the involvement of three men, seen repeatedly using Sandy's card. Moreover, a fourth individual, a woman, emerged as a suspect after using Sandy's card at a clothing store and pharmacy.

As new leads surfaced, the state police shifted their operations to Rochester. Investigator Bowling revealed their reliance on surveillance footage, though one tape offered no clarity. In a parallel effort, local dog groomers and veterinarians were alerted to be on the lookout for Jessie, easily identifiable by her blue canvas collar.

Local hospitals were alerted to keep an eye out for any pregnant women matching Sandy's description. This was a critical move, considering Sandy's advanced stage of pregnancy, and the likelihood that she might seek medical assistance.

The breakthrough in the case came on Saturday, June 11th, when investigators successfully identified the three young men from Rochester who had been using Sandy's credit card. However, the identity of the woman involved remained a mystery. The police diligently followed up on this lead, hoping it would bring them closer to understanding Sandy's fate.

In a parallel development, a report about a dog resembling Jessie floating in the Genesee River sent investigators scrambling to the Studson Street Bridge. Fortunately, or unfortunately, the retrieved dog was not Jessie, deepening the mystery of Sandy's whereabouts.

Three days later, the tone of the investigation took a grim turn. Investigator Bowling publicly expressed his belief that Sandy had likely fallen victim to foul play. The fact that Sandy had missed her own baby shower, an event she would have undoubtedly cherished, supported this somber hypothesis.

As the search continued, investigators were directed to two new areas: near the Panorama Plaza in the town of Penfield, about 14 miles northwest, and around the intersection of Hudson Avenue and Reed Park in Rochester. These locations were identified through the interrogation of the three men who had used Sandy's credit card. They claimed to have received the card from a friend, who in turn had found Sandy's wallet discarded in a row of hedges near North Street. Although these men admitted to using the card illegally, they insisted they had no connection to Sandy's disappearance. The police, following these leads, interviewed the child and family who found the wallet, gradually ruling out the men's involvement in Sandy's actual disappearance.

The search took a significant turn when Sandy's purse and Jessie's dog collar and tags were discovered in a dumpster behind a car wash at Panorama Plaza. This discovery suggested that whoever was responsible for Sandy's disappearance might have used the car wash to clean evidence from their vehicle. The theory that Sandy likely got into a car with someone she knew, given Jessie's known reluctance to be friendly with strangers, gained traction.

This lead indicated a possible trajectory of the suspect, moving from Macedon, through Penfield, and into Rochester. The media began to draw comparisons between the search efforts for Sandy and those for Kaylee Poulton. While Kaylee's disappearance received extensive coverage and a flood of tips, Sandy's case seemed to fade into the background, with minimal public attention and fewer tips.

Investigator Bowling, while acknowledging the disparity in media coverage and public interest, hinted at the challenges posed by Sandy's case. The delay in reporting her missing and the lack of substantial leads made the investigation particularly difficult.

By the end of June, with avenues of investigation dwindling, the focus shifted back to those closest to Sandy. Her parents, Dominic and Nancy, moved into her duplex apartment in hopes of being closer to the investigation and possibly being there if Sandy returned. Despite the growing frustration and pain, they clung to hope for any positive development.

In a renewed effort, investigators launched a helicopter search covering the areas between Sandy's apartment and the car wash where her belongings were found. Yet, this too yielded no significant leads. The investigative team was scaled down, but Sandy's family offered a substantial reward for information leading to her location.

As July began, Sandra Karaoke, a friend of Sandy's, spearheaded a campaign to bring more attention to Sandy's case. She highlighted the stark difference in media coverage between Sandy's and Kaylee's disappearances. Eastman Kodak, Sandy's employer, funded the production of 1,000 missing person flyers, but the disparity in public attention and media coverage remained a source of frustration and anguish.

Investigator Bowling acknowledged the difference in the public's response to the two cases. While Kaylee's case generated an overwhelming number of tips, Sandy's case struggled to gain similar traction.

On a seemingly ordinary Wednesday, July 6th, a ripple of hope stirred in the ongoing investigation into Sandra Sollie's disappearance when the Newark Police Department received an anonymous tip. The caller claimed to have seen something deeply unsettling – a woman's body floating in the Erie Canal, the same canal near where Sandy was last seen. Responding to this potential lead, four state police divers embarked on an exhaustive six-hour search in the canal's murky waters, hoping to uncover something that would lead them to Sandy. However, their efforts were in vain as no remains were found. The investigators publicly appealed for the anonymous caller to provide a more precise location, but to their dismay, the caller never came forward again.

While this lead ultimately fizzled out, the commitment to finding Sandy remained undeterred. Sandra Karaoke, a friend of Sandy's, continued her relentless campaign to keep the case in the public eye. She spearheaded the production of more flyers, which spread not only from Macedon to Rochester but also reached the surrounding Buffalo areas and cascaded down the Eastern Seaboard. Despite these extensive efforts, the influx of tips was disappointingly scant, and the case increasingly grew cold.

As summer waned, August brought a date heavy with significance and sorrow for Sandy's family – August 15th, the week Sandy's son was due. Instead of celebrating the joy of new life, they were confronted with the harrowing possibility of mourning two losses. Sandy's sister-in-law Kathy shared with the media the emotional turmoil the family was experiencing during this time, a poignant reflection of their ongoing struggle between hope and despair.

During the investigation, a critical question repeatedly surfaced: who was the father of Sandy's unborn child? This question was not as frequently addressed in the media as one might expect, given the potential motive it could provide for Sandy's disappearance. A study by the Maryland Department of Health and Mental Hygiene highlighted a stark reality: homicide is a leading cause of death among pregnant women, accounting for a significant percentage of fatalities.

Sandy's friends and her sister Donna had shared with investigators that Sandy had confided in them about the child's paternity – her ex-husband Ralph. They revealed that Sandy and Ralph had rekindled their relationship post-divorce, and it was during this time that Sandy became pregnant. While there weren't any public statements from Ralph denying this claim, his overall public statements were few.

The situation took another turn in mid-August when Ralph spoke to the media. He had been questioned multiple times by investigators and had provided them with phone and bank records accounting for his whereabouts around the time of Sandy's disappearance. Although he acknowledged seeing Sandy on the morning of May 23rd, he refused a polygraph test on the advice of his lawyer and also denied police permission to search his property.

Ralph's lawyer later emphasized his client's cooperation, downplaying any wrongdoing on his part. However, Investigator Bowling stated that while Ralph had spoken to Macedon police, he hadn't conversed with the state police. Contradictorily, Lieutenant Barry Chase of the New York State Police clarified that Ralph had been interviewed but was never officially considered a suspect.

In September 1994, a tragic event unfolded – the murder of 24-year-old Vicky Sollie, Ralph's sister and Sandy's former sister-in-law, in a double homicide near Penfield. This incident briefly redirected the investigation's focus, wondering if there was any link to Sandy's disappearance. However, after the arrest of the responsible teenagers, it became clear there was no connection, as Vicky and Sandy had never been close.

As the year neared its end, another search was conducted along the Erie Canal, this time involving a helicopter scouring a 10-mile stretch. Like previous efforts, this search yielded no new clues. State Police Investigator Robert Fennis later expressed that they had thoroughly checked the canal, and it was unlikely that further searches would reveal anything new. Chief Ellis of Macedon also acknowledged the lack of leads, emphasizing the growing coldness of the case.

Meanwhile, the investigation into the abduction of Kaylee Poulton was experiencing a similar fate. Once a hotbed of tips and leads, it too had dwindled to a trickle. Both investigations, though still active, were left hoping for new information to emerge from the community.

In Kaylee's case, this hope would eventually bear fruit, but not for nearly two more years. Sandy's case, however, remained shrouded in mystery, a haunting reminder of the unanswered questions and enduring pain that lingered in the hearts of those who knew and loved Sandra Sollie.

In August of 1996, a harrowing chapter unfolded in the case of four-year-old Kaylee Poulton's disappearance. Mark Christie, a former security guard who had once lived near the Poulton family, shockingly confessed to the authorities that he had been responsible for the abduction and murder of young Kaylee on the night she vanished. Christie, who had eerily remarked on Kaylee's beauty to her parents in the past, then chillingly led the investigators to where he had hidden her remains – in a massive, thirty-thousand-gallon water tank.

The confession and the grim discovery sent ripples of shock and sorrow throughout the community. Kaylee's mother, Judy Gifford, shared her haunting suspicion about Christie with the South Coast Today news. Despite the lack of concrete evidence initially pointing towards Christie, her instincts had eerily singled him out as a suspect, a suspicion that, in the end, tragically proved correct.

For Sandy's family, the closure of Kaylee's case brought a complex mixture of emotions. While they felt deep sympathy for the Poultons, they also experienced a poignant sense of longing. The resolution in Kaylee's case only accentuated the gaping void in their own hearts – the absence of answers in Sandy's disappearance. Nancy, Sandy's mother, poignantly expressed the family's heartache, emphasizing the unbearable weight of not knowing Sandy's fate.

Around the same time, Richard Ingram, a seasoned private investigator and former corrections officer, was moved by the news of Christie's arrest and its mention of Sandy's unresolved case. He reached out to Sandy's family, offering to assist in the search for just one dollar. His involvement coincided with a reinvigoration of the investigation, as a new team from the state police's Violent Crime Interdiction Team was assigned to reexamine Sandy's case with a fresh perspective.

In October of 1996, the renewed investigation efforts included bringing tracking dogs from Canada to meticulously re-scan the areas along the Erie

Canal and other key locations linked to Sandy's disappearance. Despite this renewed vigor and extensive search efforts, no major breakthroughs emerged.

Each year, on the anniversary of Sandy's disappearance, Richard Ingram would visit West Wayne Plaza, one of the last places Sandy was seen. He handed out flyers and spoke passionately about Sandy's case, determined to keep her memory alive and the search active. Ingram emphasized the need to maintain pressure on the investigation and famously advised looking into close acquaintances before strangers in cases like Sandy's.

The years passed with no significant progress in the case, bringing with them sorrowful milestones. On January 3rd, 2008, nearly 14 years after Sandy's disappearance, her mother, Nancy, passed away at the age of 80. The loss of her daughter had cast a profound shadow over Nancy's later years, marked by declining health and a withdrawal from public life. Donna, Sandy's sister, reflected on the profound change in their mother, noting the diminishing frequency of her smiles and laughter, now often replaced by tears and sadness.

Sandy's nephew, Michael Glow, who was 22 at the time of her disappearance, felt a deep connection to his aunt and shared in the family's frustration over the lack of progress in the case. In May 2014, he organized a candlelight vigil, releasing balloons with heartfelt messages for Sandy. It was a poignant event, offering a semblance of closure in the absence of a formal goodbye.

Tragedy struck again on October 3rd when Sandy's father, Dominic, passed away at 89. In a touching gesture, Sandy's name was etched on her parents' tombstone, symbolically uniting the family.

A significant development occurred in October 2016 when police finally gained access to a property on Wide Rick Road in Macedon, previously owned by Ralph Sollie, Sandy's ex-husband. The property had been a point of interest since Sandy's disappearance, but Ralph had denied access for a search. With the property under new ownership, the police were granted permission to conduct a thorough search with canine units and divers. New York State Trooper Mark O'Donnell conveyed the intention of the search – to seek closure for Sandy's family and to bring the case to a resolution. This development reignited a flicker of hope in the decades-long quest for answers in Sandra Sollie's mysterious disappearance.

Maya Millete

aya Millete's extraordinary journey started in the Philippines, where she was born on May 1, 1981, as the beloved fifth child among six siblings. Growing up in a dynamic and loving family, Maya demonstrated an early flair for academics, distinguishing herself as a keen learner eager for new experiences.

In 1995, a new chapter began for Maya and her family as they moved to Honolulu, Hawaii. Attending Radford High School, Maya flourished in this new, culturally rich setting. She engaged enthusiastically in drama and dance, showcasing her artistic talents and elegance.

Graduating at the age of 17, Maya entered the workforce at a McDonald's restaurant. It was in this lively environment that she met Larry Millete. Their connection was immediate, leading to a blossoming relationship. By 19, Maya was poised for further academic adventures.

Pursuing higher education, Maya attended the University of Hawaii, majoring in International Studies. Concurrently, Larry began Naval training in Virginia. Despite their separate paths, their bond remained strong, and they eventually relocated to Southern California. Maya excelled academically and professionally, graduating with honors and joining the US Navy as a civilian contract specialist in San Diego, reflecting her dedication and ambition.

Maya and Larry, now financially stable, decided to grow their family. In

2010, they welcomed their daughter Lara, followed by Milani and their son Lazarus in 2016. Maya's approach to motherhood mirrored her approach to life: passionate, devoted, and always striving to provide the best for her children.

An avid lover of the outdoors, Maya's adventurous spirit was evident in her hobbies which included hiking, biking, off-roading, camping, and traveling with her children. She was a constant presence at their school events, always supportive and encouraging. Maya's generosity extended beyond her family; she was known for her charitable work, often donating school supplies to children in rural areas of the Philippines during her visits.

Maya, a woman of many talents, had a special affinity for music. Self-taught on guitar and piano, her home was often filled with the sweet sounds of her playing. By January 2021, at 39, Maya was residing in Chula Vista, California, with her family. Yet, her marriage was undergoing strain, largely due to Larry's knowledge of an alleged affair. His reaction was one of control and paranoia.

Friends of Maya described a home life marked by tension and fear. Larry's behavior reportedly grew unpredictable and allegedly abusive towards Maya. Concerned for her safety, a friend offered her a refuge. Maya was resolute in her decision to leave this unstable environment for her children's well-being.

January 7th marked a significant yet unassuming event: a CCTV camera in a tranquil Chula Vista neighborhood recorded Maya returning home around 5 p.m. She had just consulted a divorce lawyer, signaling deep personal distress. After this moment, Maya vanished from public view, sparking a mystery that deeply affected her community and family.

The following day, January 8th, was enveloped in eerie circumstances. Early in the morning, around 6:45 a.m., a black SUV, likely driven by Larry, left their residence. It returned later that evening, around 6 p.m. The events of those

12 hours are shrouded in mystery.

Maya, known for her timely communications and strong sibling bonds, suddenly fell silent. This unusual lack of contact immediately worried her family. They were in the midst of planning a birthday outing at Big Bear Lake for Maya's eldest daughter, set for January 10th. But Maya's sudden halt in communication about the trip was deeply troubling.

Concerned, Maya's brother visited her Chula Vista home for clarity. There, Larry told a disturbing tale: Maya had supposedly been in a room alone since the night before after an argument. Larry mentioned a day trip to Solona Beach with his son, and upon returning, he claimed Maya was still shut in the room.

The family's anxiety intensified. On January 9th, they returned, desperate for answers. Larry eventually let them check the room, which they found eerily empty, with no sign of Maya. Larry casually suggested she might have gone hiking, yet her car was still parked at home, adding to the mystery.

At midnight, driven by fear and desperation, Maya's sister Mari Chris reported her missing. The details were unsettling: Maya's last known communication was at 8:15 p.m. on January 7th, and by 1:25 a.m. on January 8th, her phone was off the network. Its last detected location was ominously close to their Chula Vista neighborhood.

The search for Maya transformed into an extensive operation. Teams of police and volunteers tirelessly scoured diverse terrains - forests, creeks, waterways, and even deserted areas. This monumental effort spread across months, reaching places like Mount San Miguel State Park, Glamis San Dunes, Otay Lake, National City, and an abandoned golf course in Chula Vista. But Maya remained elusive, her fate a persistent enigma.

As the investigation intensified, the authorities escalated their actions. On

January 23rd, they conducted the first of a staggering 67 searches at the Millete home. They uncovered a concerning array of 16 firearms owned by Larry, including two illegally possessed guns. More troubling was the unaccounted-for weaponry, which Larry claimed he had loaned out. This led to a gun violence restraining order against Larry in May 2021. The decision was influenced by alarming photos of the Millete children with rifles and their knowledge of his gun safe's code. The children's safety became a critical focus.

The investigation's scope expanded with the FBI and the Naval Criminal Investigative Service joining in, particularly analyzing the family's vehicles. Hopes fluctuated with the discovery of skeletal remains in Orange County. The community, Maya's family, and law enforcement held their collective breath, wondering if this could be the crucial clue in Maya's case.

However, this beacon of hope dimmed when it turned out the remains were from an animal. This devastating turn deepened the sorrow of Maya's family, who had been holding onto every thread of hope in their quest to find her.

In the wake of Maya's disappearance, her family stood resolutely in the spotlight, advocating for her return. They engaged with the media fervently, appealing to the public for any information. Their commitment to keeping Maya's story alive was unwavering, as seen in the widespread distribution of flyers and posters, each adorned with Maya's image - a poignant symbol of the missing mother, sister, and daughter.

The passing of Maya's daughter's birthday, an occasion she would never have missed, further solidified the family's fears of foul play. A disturbing development arose when a neighbor's CCTV captured a chilling sequence: eight gunshots echoing from the Millete home around 9:57 p.m. on January 7th. An audio clip was publicly shared, marked by a sinister backdrop of dogs barking, while the video remained undisclosed, likely to protect the investigation and the neighbor's identity.

Adding to the intrigue, neighbors' CCTV later showed an unusual sight around 10:34 p.m.: Larry engaging in backyard play with his children, an oddity given the cold night.

Throughout the search efforts, Larry's absence was conspicuous; he did not join any search parties for Maya. In the ensuing weeks and months, he severed all contact between Maya's family and their three children.

The police initially withheld judgment. There was a possibility that Maya, after an argument, might have left voluntarily to cool off. However, this theory lacked concrete evidence, with no CCTV footage showing her leaving the premises.

Larry emerged as a key figure in the investigation and soon retained legal counsel, halting his cooperation with the police. During their probe, the police gathered testimonies from Maya's relatives, including her sister, who recalled a recent camping trip. There, Maya and Larry had argued persistently. Alarmingly, Larry was suspected of inquiring about the man Maya was allegedly seeing and possibly contemplating hiring a hitman.

A disturbing revelation came from Maya's family. They shared with the police that Maya had once ominously stated that if anything were to happen to her, Larry should be considered responsible. On July 22nd, over half a year after Maya vanished, the police formally recognized Larry as a person of interest. Their affidavit suggested they believed Larry had taken Maya's life between the night of January 7th and the morning of January 8th, and then concealed her body.

Larry's account to the police was consistent yet suspicious. He maintained that after their argument on January 7th, Maya secluded herself in their bedroom, never to be seen again. He claimed to have spent January 8th at the beach, and upon returning, he thought he heard Maya upstairs. However, his unclear whereabouts on January 6th, 7th, and 8th, absence from work, and an 11-hour period on January 8th when his phone was off raised red flags for investigators.

Security footage captured Larry's car being driven in a peculiar manner at their home, backing up the driveway towards the garage and out of the camera's view. This led to speculation about whether he might have been loading or unloading something from his car, adding another layer of mystery to the case.

In the thorough search of their residence, police confiscated Larry's phone and discovered a puzzling fact: all texts between him and Maya had been deleted. Larry rationalized this by saying he needed to clear storage space, but investigators were skeptical, knowing that text messages don't typically consume much storage.

The probe into Larry's online activity revealed more ominous aspects. His search history included queries about substances and plants that could render someone unconscious, suggesting a potentially malicious intent. Searches about his wife's decreasing interest in him also surfaced. Most unsettling, however, was Larry's frequent visits to websites offering spellcasting services from September 2020 to January 2021.

Investigators learned that Larry had been fervently buying spells aimed at Maya. These spells were alarming in nature, with requests like causing Maya harm, confining her to the house, and even wishing for her to have an accident. His fixation on controlling Maya seemed to reach its peak with what looked like a shrine dedicated to her, allegedly adorned with his blood. Intriguingly, Larry's purchase of these spells stopped abruptly around the time of Maya's disappearance on January 9th, coinciding with his request to the spellcasters to cease their activities.

In the subsequent custody battle over Maya's children, Larry maintained his belief that Maya was still alive, suggesting she had left of her own accord, as she had allegedly done before. He described her as unpredictable and prone to isolating herself in their bedroom. He also accused Maya's family of defaming him, implying their allegations were part of a slander campaign.

Larry's financial transactions added another layer of suspicion. He made a significant withdrawal from his bank, fueling theories that he might have been planning an escape to elude legal consequences. On October 19, 2021, Larry Millete was taken into custody, facing charges of murdering Maya and illegal possession of an assault weapon. He entered a plea of not guilty.

The legal proceedings were riddled with complexities. Initially, Larry was prohibited from contacting his children, except through legal counsel. Nonetheless, he breached this restriction by communicating with them during calls to his parents. Concurrently, Maya's sister and parents pursued custody of the children. While they secured expanded visitation, the children's primary custody was with their paternal grandparents.

As the trial date approached, concerns about Larry's mental fitness for trial surfaced. A psychiatric assessment in June 2022 deemed him competent. The trial, scheduled to begin on January 16, 2024, has already been delayed by financial constraints and a motion from Larry's attorney to withdraw from the case.

Three years have elapsed since Maya's disappearance, and her fate remains a mystery. Her family, the local community, and law enforcement continue their quest for clarity in this perplexing and tragic case. The upcoming trial offers a ray of hope for uncovering the truth, but the question of whether justice will be realized in Maya Millete's case is yet to be answered.

Elizabeth Prescott

On a warm April evening in Callaway, Florida, a charming community just outside Panama City, 23-year-old Coy Prescott and his 19-year-old wife, Elizabeth Iris Prescott, known fondly as Beth, were browsing the aisles of their local Walmart. The next day was a significant one – Coy's 24th birthday, and Beth was on a mission to prepare the perfect celebration dinner. Earlier in the day, she had sought advice for making the family's beloved meatloaf recipe, a favorite of Coy's, and for the birthday cake, she planned to decorate it with blue icing, featuring the number '6' in honor of Coy's favorite race car driver, Mark Martin.

The couple's marriage was a recent chapter in their lives, having been married for just two months. They lived in a conveniently located apartment near Walmart, which was especially handy since they didn't own a car.

Beth, born on October 5, 1984, had a background rich with personal connections and experiences. After graduating from Rutherford High School, she formed a close relationship with her stepmother, Donna Pagliaicetti, who became a significant figure of support and guidance in her life. Beth's father, Vincent Pagliaicetti, viewed his daughter with a mix of affection and concern, recognizing her youthful naivety and optimistic outlook on life.

Beth's journey to marriage wasn't straightforward. Just a year earlier, she was engaged to Eric Moore, but that relationship ended in December, paving the way for her union with Coy in February. The details of when Beth and

Coy's romance began are not clearly known. Beth's diary entries during this period reflect her contentment and the sense of peace she found in married life, contrasting with her more tumultuous past. These writings illustrate a young woman embracing a new phase of life filled with love, hope, and new beginnings.

On the morning of April 30, 2004, in the small town of Callaway, Florida, the day began like any other for Coy Prescott and his wife, Beth. Coy was preparing to leave for work, and in their brief morning exchange, Beth reminded him to call her an hour before his shift ended to coordinate their dinner plans. Coy departed their home around 5:45 a.m., not realizing it would be the last time he would hear his wife's voice. Beth vanished that day, leaving behind a mystery that would puzzle the community and haunt Coy.

Later that day, adhering to their plan, Coy called Beth, expecting to discuss their evening meal. However, his calls went unanswered. Puzzled and increasingly concerned, Coy left messages, hoping Beth would return them shortly. Upon finishing his workday, Coy returned home around 4 p.m., only to be met with an unsettling silence. The apartment was empty; Beth was nowhere to be found. A lone damp towel in the bathroom and the absence of $50 indicated Beth had been home earlier. Curiously, someone had checked Coy's first voicemail, but the second message remained unheard. This inconsistency in the answering machine's status baffled everyone.

As the night passed without Beth's return, Coy's concern escalated. By the next morning, with no sign of Beth, Coy reached out to Donna Pagliacetti, Beth's stepmother, hoping for any clue. Donna, equally perplexed, hadn't heard from Beth and advised Coy to involve the police. With a heavy heart, Coy contacted the authorities, initiating a baffling missing person case.

Coy recounted to the police their last known activities - a trip to Walmart the evening before Beth's disappearance and their brief morning conversation. Despite multiple witnesses confirming their presence at the store, the trail went cold thereafter. The police diligently pursued every lead, subpoenaing phone records and scrutinizing security footage from Walmart, but to no avail. The couple's apartment yielded no signs of forced entry or struggle, deepening the mystery. It seemed as though Beth had left of her own volition, taking only her purse, the clothes she was wearing, and the missing $50.

Dave Kania of the Bay County Sheriff's Department was particularly troubled by the case. In his conversation with journalist Anthony Cormier, Kania pointed out the peculiar fact that all of Beth's clothing remained at the apartment, an oddity for someone planning to leave. He delved into Beth's journals, searching for clues in her personal writings. Despite the evident emotional ups and downs in her entries, nothing suggested a troubled marriage, a desire to flee, or any sense of danger. People close to Beth had also not noticed anything amiss in her behavior or expressions.

The case was labeled as a missing person under suspicious circumstances due to the lack of evidence of any wrongdoing. Beth's past, including a brief runaway episode as a teenager and her continued communication with an ex-boyfriend even after her marriage, added layers to the investigation. The police interviewed the ex-boyfriend, who, along with Coy, voluntarily underwent a polygraph test, which both passed.

Another individual emerged in the investigation, a mysterious man whose connection to Beth remained unclear. Despite his claim of not knowing Beth, police discovered two photographs of her in his wallet, deepening the intrigue. However, no substantial leads or evidence surfaced from these interactions.

The baffling disappearance of Beth Prescott left her family, Coy, and the community grappling with questions. Beth's parents, Vincent and Donna, found themselves in a whirlwind of confusion and concern, recalling Beth's previous impulsive actions but unable to reconcile them with her current disappearance. The case remained shrouded in mystery, with no conclusive evidence pointing to what happened to Beth Prescott that fateful April day.

On May 6, exactly one week after Beth's mysterious disappearance, a team of detectives descended upon the Abalone Apartments, where Beth and Coy Prescott resided. Their mission was thorough and meticulous: to comb through every inch of the couple's apartment for any clue that might shed light on Beth's whereabouts. As they sifted through the couple's possessions, the inventory revealed telltale signs of a sudden departure - Beth's cell phone was left behind, alongside most of her clothing, items one wouldn't normally leave without.

Determined to leave no stone unturned, the detectives painstakingly read through Beth's diaries, poring over each page in search of any hint or clue. Despite their thorough examination, the diaries yielded nothing unusual or suspicious.

The search extended beyond the confines of the apartment. Abalone Apartments was nestled amidst a vast expanse of woods dotted with several ponds, an area that beckoned further investigation. This prompted the involvement of Bay County Search and Rescue, a team well-versed in navigating and scrutinizing such terrain. Their search was extensive: dragging bodies of water, conducting meticulous foot searches with the aid of K9 units. Despite their exhaustive efforts, no evidence linked to Beth was uncovered.

As the year progressed, updates on the investigation trickled down to Coy, Donna, and Vincent, but they brought little solace. October arrived, a month that used to herald a celebration for Beth's birthday, now transformed into a somber time filled with dread, fear, and anguish. Beth's 20th birthday passed, marked not with joy and festivity, but with a heavy cloud of sorrow hanging over those who loved her.

Donna, in her moments of despair, likened their ordeal to a living nightmare. Despite being thankful for the police's persistent efforts, the passage of time only amplified their anguish. The police department, through a spokesperson, reassured the family and the public that Beth's case remained a priority, with each detective committed to unraveling the mystery of her disappearance.

January 2005 brought a significant yet disheartening development: nine months after Beth vanished, the police announced they were treating her case as a likely homicide. The inactivity in her bank accounts and social security number since her disappearance only deepened the suspicions surrounding her fate.

Detective Kania, leading the investigation, posited that had Beth chosen to leave of her own accord, she would have likely made contact with someone by now. This announcement, while stark, did not yield any suspects.

The focus of the investigation began to shift, honing in on people within Beth's close circle. Subpoenas for phone records of Beth and her family were issued, and attention turned towards Eric Moore, Beth's former fiancé, who had ended their engagement. Eric's role in Beth's past was scrutinized, particularly given the revelation that he and Beth had continued seeing each other, an affair that escalated after her marriage to Coy. Despite his cooperation with the investigation and the return of the engagement ring being chalked up to a morbid coincidence, Eric was never charged in connection to Beth's disappearance.

Throughout the years, Coy Prescott remained a figure of interest but consistently cooperated with the authorities. Despite avoiding media attention, Coy was interviewed a second time in May 2005, where he expressed suspicions of Beth's possible whereabouts with Eric. Captain Jimmy Stanford of the Bay County Sheriff's Department noted the intense nature of this interrogation, revealing Coy's emotional strain but ultimately, it yielded no breakthrough.

The years passed, and in 2012, eight years after Beth's vanishing, CrimeStoppers organized a rally at the Callaway Walmart in an effort to reignite public interest in the case. It was there that Donna Pagliacetti, standing at the podium, made a heartfelt plea for information regarding her stepdaughter.

She emphasized how even the smallest detail could bring an end to years of unanswered questions.

Donna and Vincent, speaking to reporters, confessed that time had done little to heal their wounds. The absence of answers meant Beth was always present in their thoughts, an enduring shadow in their lives.

At the rally, volunteers, family members, and investigators joined forces, distributing flyers to shoppers. Their hope was to spark a memory, a clue, anything that could lead to solving the enduring mystery of what happened to Elizabeth Prescott.

As the perplexing case of Elizabeth Prescott's disappearance continued to unfold, a new and intriguing figure emerged, casting a shadow over the investigation. Ivan Ferrer-Perdomo, a man with a daunting criminal record that spanned nearly 15 years, including a conviction for murder, entered the fray as a potential suspect. His notoriety in the criminal world was well-known, but it was a shocking revelation from inside prison walls that brought him into the orbit of Beth's case. Inmates reported that Perdomo had bragged about committing a heinous act – the murder of Elizabeth Prescott.

According to the chilling tales circulating in prison, Perdomo claimed that Beth had visited his residence on 23rd Street, a mere eight-minute drive from the Abalone Apartments where she lived, under the guise of purchasing drugs. In a harrowing turn of events, Perdomo alleged that he ambushed and killed Beth upon her arrival.

The investigators, upon learning of these allegations, swiftly confronted Perdomo. Faced with the accusations, he became reticent and immediately sought legal counsel, rendering further questioning ineffective. The investigators delved deeper into Perdomo's past, yet they found no tangible link between him and Beth Prescott. Furthermore, critical inconsistencies in Perdomo's narrative became apparent, clashing with key details known exclusively to the investigators.

One theory proposed by an investigator suggested that Perdomo, perhaps seeking notoriety or attention, might have fabricated his involvement. This theory was based on the possibility that Perdomo had seen Elizabeth's picture on cold case cards circulated in the prison and decided to concoct a story for his own purposes.

In 2021, Perdomo resurfaced in the public eye under dramatic circumstances. A violent altercation erupted between him and a friend, leading to a 911 call. As the police arrived, Perdomo, possibly fearing a parole violation, hastily concealed himself. Once the officers departed, the situation escalated rapidly. Armed with a knife, Perdomo launched another attack on his victim, tying him up, and threatening his life if he made any sound. He then proceeded to rob him, taking his money and car, and fled to another state.

However, his flight from justice was short-lived. The U.S. Marshals, adept in their pursuit, swiftly apprehended Perdomo. He faced a litany of charges including robbery with a deadly weapon, aggravated battery, false impris- onment, grand theft of a motor vehicle, and tampering with a victim or witness. Ultimately, a grand jury found him guilty on all counts, resulting in a life sentence. Despite these convictions and his alleged confession within the prison walls, Ivan Ferrer-Perdomo has never been officially charged in connection with the disappearance of Elizabeth Prescott.

In the ongoing and enigmatic case of Beth Prescott's disappearance, the police have meticulously developed three principal theories in their quest to uncover what happened to her. Each theory, while plausible, opens up a labyrinth of possibilities and unanswered questions, deepening the mystery surrounding her sudden vanishing.

The first theory posits that Beth, driven by unknown reasons, made the drastic decision to abandon her life and start anew, possibly in a foreign country. This theory, however, stumbles over several practical hurdles. Beth's sudden departure lacked any form of logistical planning; she didn't have a car, making the journey to the nearest airport or any distant location seemingly improbable. This scenario also contradicts the known aspects of her life and personality, casting doubt on its likelihood.

The second theory speculates that Beth may have been abducted, either close to or within her apartment complex. Considering her outgoing and sociable nature, it's conceivable that her abductor could have been an acquaintance or even a stranger who took advantage of her trusting disposition. This theory opens up a multitude of potential scenarios, each as chilling as the next, revolving around the idea of an unexpected and sinister encounter leading to her abduction.

The third theory suggests a more spontaneous occurrence. Perhaps Beth, in preparation for the celebration with Coy, decided to make a quick trip to the nearby Walmart for additional ingredients. Tragically, this theory proposes that along her route, she encountered an unforeseen danger – perhaps an individual with malicious intent – preventing her from ever reaching the store.

Amidst these theories, Vincent and Donna Pagliacetti, Beth's parents, struggle to accept the notion of her willingly starting a new life elsewhere. They lean towards the more grim possibilities, fearing that Beth's trusting nature may have inadvertently put her in harm's way, making her susceptible to foul play. They find it entirely plausible that Beth, in her characteristic openness, might have unwittingly allowed a stranger into her home or entered someone's car, setting the stage for her mysterious disappearance.

As the years roll on, Vincent and Donna grapple with the relentless pain and heartache that Beth's sudden disappearance has etched into their lives. The lack of closure only compounds their suffering, but they remain steadfast in their grief, honoring their daughter's memory, continually searching for answers, and holding onto the faint glimmer of hope for a resolution.

In a poignant twist of fate, in 2018, the Abalone Apartments, the last known residence of Beth and Coy Prescott, were ravaged and ultimately demolished by the devastating forces of Hurricane Michael. The apartments, a silent witness to Beth's last known moments, now lay in ruins, swallowed by the relentless march of time and nature. This destruction erased the physical remnants of the last place where Beth was seen alive, adding a somber, almost symbolic layer to the already heartrending mystery of her disappearance.

Mark Himebaugh

Mark Joseph Himebaugh's story begins in the quiet, picturesque town of Delhaven, New Jersey. Born on May 23, 1980, Mark grew up in this small community nestled at the southern tip of New Jersey, where the serene waters of the Delaware Bay kiss the shore. The Himebaugh family home, a cozy abode on the 200 block of Sun Ray Road, was filled with the typical bustle and warmth of family life. There, Mark lived with his mother, Maureen, his father, Jody, and his older brother, Matthew.

The Himebaugh household, like many, had its share of challenges. Mark's father, Jody, was a man of many trades, constantly shifting from one job to the next, while his mother, Maureen, juggled her roles as a waitress and a house cleaner. Jody, a man who seemed to place a higher value on leisure than on financial prudence, owned both a boat and a camping trailer, despite the family's tight financial situation.

In March of 1991, a significant shift occurred in the Himebaugh family dynamics. Jody and Maureen decided to separate. Jody moved into an apartment close by, while Mark and Matthew stayed with their mother. During this time, Mark faced his own set of struggles. He often found it difficult to manage his emotions, exhibiting frequent outbursts of anger and frustration when things didn't align with his expectations. His challenges were further compounded when he was diagnosed with obsessive-compulsive disorder, for which he received mental health counseling. As part of his educational journey, Mark attended the Cape May County Alternative Middle School.

Life threw another curveball at Mark in mid-October 1991 when he broke his left foot during a playful day at the playground. This injury would later play a significant role in the events to come.

Now, let's delve into the crucial timeline of Mark's mysterious disappearance. On the afternoon of Monday, November 25, 1991, Mark returned home from school on the bus around 2:15 pm. Shortly thereafter, around 2:40 pm, his mother Maureen arrived back from the supermarket to find Mark relaxing on the couch, engrossed in a television program.

However, the tranquility of the day was soon disrupted. Around 3 pm, fire-fighters rushed to extinguish a brush fire in the marshlands, approximately a quarter-mile south of the Himebaugh residence. This event captivated the local community; in a town where excitement was scarce, the spectacle of a fire drew a crowd, including young Mark, who eagerly climbed up his father's amateur radio tower for a better view.

Seizing the moment, Mark asked his mother if he could get a closer look at the fire. He switched his footwear to a worn pair of hand-me-down sneakers, mindful of his still-recovering broken foot, but not opting for any special protective gear. As he set off towards the fire, a neighbor approached Maureen, seeking a lift to an automotive repair facility. Maureen agreed, briefly notifying Mark of her departure and receiving a simple, "Okay, Mom" in response – tragically, these would be the last words she ever heard from her son.

The brush fire led to roadblocks and diversions, elongating Maureen's errand from a mere 15 minutes to about 40 minutes. Upon her return around 4 pm, Mark was nowhere to be seen. Frantic, Maureen searched the area to no avail. By 5 PM, though the fire was extinguished, Mark remained missing. Growing increasingly alarmed, Maureen contacted the police at around 6 pm, sparking a vast search operation involving police, firefighters, and volunteers.

The search took a grim turn at about 8 PM when authorities discovered a sneaker on the beach, just 225 feet from the Himebaugh home. It was Mark's left sneaker, the one protecting his injured foot. Police dogs traced the scent from the sneaker northward to Roosevelt Boulevard, but there, the trail went cold.

The police, speculating that Mark might be hiding in the marshland and afraid of repercussions, called off the search at 1:30 am, hoping he would emerge on his own. But dawn broke with no sign of Mark, and the search resumed on Tuesday, November 26th.

In a turn of events that would raise eyebrows, Mark's father, Jody, went to work as usual on that fateful Tuesday, a decision the police and community found disturbingly indifferent under the circumstances. Jody explained his absence from the search by citing a lack of insurance for his vehicle, a claim corroborated by his employer, who confirmed Jody's presence at work on November 25, the day Mark vanished. Later that evening, after performing with his barbershop quartet, Jody finally joined the search efforts, but by then, hours had slipped away, and the mystery of Mark's disappearance only deepened.

On the chilly evening of November 25, 1991, the small town of Delhaven, New Jersey, was under the shadow of a young boy's mysterious disappearance. The missing boy was Mark Joseph Himebaugh, and the search for him had mobilized the community. However, Jody, Mark's father, did not join the search effort until 9:30 pm, hours after the boy was reported missing. This delay in Jody's arrival only added to the mounting tension and mystery surrounding the case.

Meanwhile, the police were conducting their own meticulous investigations. They turned their attention to Jody's apartment, scouring it for any clue that might link him to his son's disappearance. Despite a thorough search, they found nothing incriminating. It was as though the police were searching for a needle in a haystack, with the needle being any sign of Jody's involvement or a 'Father of the Year' trophy, the latter of which was conspicuously absent given the strained relationship between father and son.

Both parents, Maureen and Jody, were interviewed by the police. Maureen painted a picture of a troubled relationship between Jody and Mark, suggesting that discipline and punishment were not uncommon in their interactions. Adding to the complexity, the police learned of allegations against Jody involving indecent exposure, though no charges were filed in connection with these claims.

In an effort to reconstruct the events of that fateful day, investigators gathered eyewitness accounts. Four teenagers reported seeing Mark around 3:20 PM, exiting the dunes onto Delaware Avenue. A couple parked on Delaware Avenue recalled seeing a red-haired boy, identifiable as Mark by his unique red shoelaces, around 3:30 PM. They watched as he walked past their vehicle, approaching a station wagon parked nearby. The station wagon was occupied by a scruffy-looking man with long hair and glasses, alongside a woman with blonde hair donning a rabbit fur coat. The man seemed to be shouting something at Mark, but the exact words were lost in the distance.

Further adding to the mystery, a guard from a nearby park on Bayshore Road reported seeing Mark with an unidentified young girl, around 9 or 10 years old, with blonde hair and a blue coat adorned with an orange stripe. This sighting, occurring between 3:40 and 4:00 PM, was the last confirmed observation of Mark. He and the mysterious girl were seen heading towards the park's playground.

Despite thorough investigations, the couple in the station wagon remained elusive, and no one could identify the young girl described by the park guard. As the case grew colder, the FBI stepped in, interviewing residents throughout the neighborhood but finding no breakthroughs.

It wasn't until February 1993 that a new lead emerged. The Philadelphia Police Department came into contact with a male sex worker who claimed to have spent time with a man named Thomas McCavage. This sex worker relayed a chilling tale: Thomas had shown him a video of a young boy with red hair being harmed, a boy who bore an uncanny resemblance to Mark. Confronting Thomas, the police noted his striking similarity to the sketch of the man seen talking to Mark near the station wagon on the day of the disappearance.

A search of Thomas's residence uncovered a cache of adult videos, but all featured consenting adults. Thomas confessed to having murderous fantasies, eerily aligning with the possible fate of Mark, yet he insisted he had never acted on these impulses. A receipt placed Thomas in Philadelphia on the day Mark disappeared, but doubts lingered about the receipt's timestamp, leaving open the possibility that Thomas could have been in Delhaven.

In 1998, Thomas was arrested and convicted for offenses against boys, receiving a prison sentence of 18 to 36 years. The case took another bizarre turn on December 27, 2010, when Crime Stoppers received an anonymous call from a phone booth in Philadelphia's Port Richmond neighborhood. The caller, claiming to be the son of a witness, suggested a man named Gilbert Patrick Marie might be connected to Mark's disappearance. However, this name led to a dead end, as the police were unable to find anyone matching that description.

As the mystery deepened, a glimmer of hope emerged in May 2023, when law enforcement announced their collaboration with a company specializing in artificial intelligence. This cutting-edge technology, adept at sifting through and connecting vast troves of data, was to be deployed in re-examining the intricate web of Mark's case. At the time of this renewed investigation, the police categorized Mark's case as a non-family abduction.

Turning to a more analytical perspective, several key elements of the case stand out for closer scrutiny. First and foremost, Mark Himebaugh was known as a vibrant, imaginative, and forward-thinking child. His inherent curiosity and zest for life make it highly improbable that he would have intentionally harmed himself or wandered off without a trace. An eleven-year-old's attempt to flee from New Jersey would undoubtedly have drawn attention, making self-initiated disappearance an unlikely scenario.

The second intriguing element involves the last known sightings of Mark. Witnesses on Delaware Avenue observed his distinctive red shoelaces, suggesting both shoes were intact at that point. This detail is critical, considering a guard at a nearby park also reported seeing Mark, this time accompanied by a mysterious girl, without mentioning any missing footwear. Consequently, it appears that Mark traveled a considerable distance, over three thousand feet, from Delaware Avenue to the park and then potentially back to the beach, where one of his sneakers was later found. The absence of struggle signs near the found sneaker, combined with the fact that police dogs tracked the scent from the sneaker over a considerable distance to Roosevelt Boulevard, only deepens the mystery. How could Mark have lost his sneaker, and under what circumstances? The cold weather that day further complicates the notion of him walking such a distance with one bare foot, raising questions about the circumstances under which the sneaker was separated from him.

The third puzzling aspect is the sighting of the young girl with Mark, described vividly by the park guard yet unrecognized by anyone else. Her existence almost seems ethereal, considering no one else reported seeing her or knew her, despite the guard's detailed description, including her blue coat with an orange stripe. This oddity raises doubts about the accuracy of the guard's memory or observation. The involvement of a young girl in a potential abduction scenario is not only unusual but also improbable, suggesting either a misremembering on the part of the witness or perhaps an entirely different, yet undiscovered, context.

In the intricate web of theories surrounding the disappearance of Mark Himebaugh, the story of the young girl seen with Mark at the park raises significant questions. Could it be that Mark never actually set foot in the park that day? The reliability of the park guard's account comes under scrutiny, particularly if his description of the girl, who seemed to vanish into thin air, was incorrect. Could he also have been mistaken about seeing Mark? This possibility casts a shadow of doubt over one of the key sightings of Mark on that fateful day.

Further delving into the day's events, the brush fire that led firefighters to reroute traffic adds another layer of complexity. The ensuing confusion and the unfamiliar routes taken by many drivers could potentially explain the interaction between Mark and the man in the station wagon. Perhaps this man, simply a passerby caught in the traffic chaos, inquired Mark for information, assuming him to be a local familiar with the situation. The presence of a woman in the vehicle with him lessens the likelihood of a premeditated abduction plan.

As for the theory linking Thomas Buckavitch to the man seen speaking with Mark near the station wagon, there are significant doubts. The resemblance between Thomas and the sketch of the man is indeed striking. However, considering Thomas' probable location in the Philadelphia area, an hour and a half drive from Delhaven, it seems less plausible that he was involved.

Nineteen years after Mark's disappearance, a mysterious call to Crime Stoppers at 3:45 AM from a phone booth in Philadelphia added yet another twist. The caller, who rang twice, provided a name for an alleged attacker that police could not trace. The possibility that the caller was fabricating not just the name but the entire account seems likely, especially considering the inaccuracies in his statements. He initially misstated the year of Mark's disappearance as 1980, the year Mark was born, a detail prominently displayed on an online flyer about the case. His later correction to 1991 and the use of Mark's full name, Mark Joseph Himebaugh, not commonly mentioned in reports but listed on the flyer, suggests he was not intimately familiar with the case and possibly aimed to mislead or cause disruption.

Mark's spirited nature is another factor to consider. His penchant for adventure and tendency to find excitement could have led to a tragic accident in the nearby marshlands or Delaware Bay. The police acknowledge this as a possibility, given the challenging terrain and the ability of such environments to conceal evidence for extended periods. The vast expanse of marshland around Mark's home is particularly notable in this context.

Reflecting on the various elements and hypotheses, three main theories emerge regarding Mark's fate: abduction by someone known to him, abduction by a stranger, or an accidental death in the local natural terrain. Of these, the most plausible seems to be abduction by an unknown individual who seized an opportune moment amidst the fire-induced chaos. This scenario mirrors that of a casual shopper turned opportunist thief during an unexpected power outage. The second most likely theory posits that Mark was taken by someone he knew, possibly someone exploiting the trust of a familiar face.

Each theory brings with it a set of complexities and unanswered questions, painting a picture of a case as mystifying as it is heartbreaking. The journey to uncover the truth about what happened to Mark Himebaugh continues, with each possibility offering a different path in the search for answers.

Brandon Helms

randon Lee Helms entered the world on the 14th of March, 1973, welcomed by his loving parents, Gail and Harry Helms. His childhood unfolded in the quaint town of Cordell, Georgia, where he grew alongside his two siblings, weaving the tapestry of a close-knit family. The year 2003 marked a significant milestone in Brandon's life as he embarked on a lifelong journey with his soulmate, Misty. Together, they embraced the joys of parenthood, raising two delightful daughters in the serene surroundings of Thomasville.

Professionally, Brandon carved out a successful career in the printing industry. His journey saw him contribute to various companies, including the Cordell Dispatch and the Valdosta Daily Times. By 2015, Brandon had embarked on a new chapter, joining the team at Home Depot, where he dedicated his skills and passion.

However, life took a twist in mid-2015 when Brandon and Misty decided to separate. Amidst this challenging phase, Brandon found solace in the companionship of his longtime friend, Monty Kilcrease. He temporarily moved into Monty's residence on Teeterville Road in Lakeland, Georgia, a location nestled in Lanier County and approximately an hour's drive from his previous abode in Thomasville. This relocation marked a period of transition for Brandon as he navigated the complexities of life's unexpected turns.

The bond between Brandon and his daughters remained unwavering. On

December 13th, a Saturday, he embraced the role of a doting father, picking up his girls from their mother for a special outing. The trio attended a Christmas company picnic hosted by Home Depot, a joyful occasion that Brandon later recounted to his mother in a phone call that evening. He shared with her the wonderful time they had, a conversation filled with laughter and fond memories. There was no hint of distress, no shadow of worry in his voice.

The following day, Sunday, saw Brandon fulfilling his fatherly duties, returning his daughters safely to their mother in Thomasville. This routine exchange appeared unremarkable, yet it unwittingly marked a poignant moment; it was the last time Brandon would be seen. The uncertainty surrounding the exact moment of his disappearance lingered, shrouded in mystery—whether it was after he left his daughters with Misty, or upon his assumed return to Monty's house.

Alarm bells rang on Monday morning when Misty, unable to reach Brandon, contacted his mother around 11:15 a.m., expressing her concern. This call set in motion a frantic search. Brandon's parents, fraught with worry, hurried to Monty's house in Lakeland, the last known haven of their son. Monty, equally perplexed, was either already at the house or en route. There, a perplexing scene awaited them: Brandon's truck sat in the driveway, while inside the house lay his cigarettes and cell phone. Mysteriously missing were his wallet, truck keys, and most alarmingly, Brandon himself.

As Brandon's parents anxiously arrived at the residence, their hearts heavy with worry, they found themselves amidst a flurry of activity. Law enforcement officers had already descended upon the scene, their presence a testament to the gravity of the situation. Tracking dogs, their keen senses attuned to the task at hand, combed the surrounding area in search of any trace of Brandon. However, despite their exhaustive efforts, the dogs failed to pick up on Brandon's scent, leaving investigators perplexed.

The circumstances surrounding Brandon's disappearance seemed to defy conventional wisdom. With his truck parked nearby, its tank filled halfway, it appeared unlikely that Brandon would have set out on foot. A man known for his aversion to the cold, especially on a dreary, rain-soaked day like December 16th, Brandon would have surely opted for the warmth and convenience of his vehicle. In the narrator's personal reflection, an empathetic connection emerges, drawing parallels between Brandon's presumed discomfort and their own aversion to chilly weather. The notion that Brandon would willingly brave such conditions on foot seemed implausible, reinforcing the notion that something more sinister may have been at play.

The response from law enforcement further underscored the seriousness of Brandon's disappearance. The Lanier County Sheriff's Office issued a "Be on the lookout" alert, emphasizing that Brandon was not a wanted criminal but rather a beloved family member whose safety was in question. Despite this concerted effort, days turned into weeks, and still, there was no word from Brandon. No eyewitnesses came forward, no trace of his whereabouts emerged from the exhaustive searches conducted across South Georgia and North Florida.

The investigation took on additional layers of complexity as polygraph tests were administered to individuals close to Brandon. Yet, the results of these tests remained undisclosed, adding a shroud of mystery to the already baffling case. Meanwhile, the legal proceedings mirrored the family's desperate search for closure. Misty, Brandon's estranged wife, sought legal recourse in 2016, attempting to have Brandon declared deceased. However, Georgia law dictated a four-year waiting period before such a declaration could be made, leaving the family in a state of limbo.

Amidst the uncertainty, Brandon's family found solace in the support of organizations like Faithfully Found, whose tireless efforts in raising awareness and mobilizing communities brought renewed hope. Candlelight vigils illuminated the night sky, a poignant reminder of Brandon's enduring presence in the hearts of those who loved him. New posters adorned public spaces, each one a beacon of possibility, beckoning for any shred of information that might lead to Brandon's whereabouts.

In the midst of the search, Brandon's character emerged as a beacon of light, described fondly as a devoted father and a cherished member of his family. His unwavering commitment to his daughters, echoed in his last poignant words to his own father, painted a portrait of a man whose love transcended all boundaries. The notion that Brandon would willingly abandon his family seemed inconceivable, challenging the very core of the investigation.

Despite the passage of time, the search for Brandon continues unabated. The Lanier County Sheriff's Office remains steadfast in their pursuit of answers, even as turnover among investigators complicates the already intricate case. Brandon's physical description, meticulously detailed, serves as a reminder of the person behind the missing poster—a son, a father, a loved one whose absence leaves an indelible void in the lives of those who hold him dear. As the years stretch on, hope flickers like a distant flame, a beacon guiding the way home for a man who vanished without a trace.

Pepita Redhair

Born amidst the vibrant culture of the Navajo Nation on August 4th, 1992, Pepita's early years were a kaleidoscope of interactions, fueled by her naturally gregarious personality. She was a beacon of warmth and charm, traits that flourished as she matured. Her interests were as varied as they were rich: from the delicate precision of her artwork to the exhilarating freedom of skateboarding. Deep in her heart, she nurtured an aspiration to shape young minds through teaching, dreaming of college to make this ambition a reality.

At 23, Pepita's path intersected with Nicholas K., known to most as Nick. Their connection was immediate, leading them swiftly into a complex romance. However, the relationship soon became enshrouded in troubles. Rumors swirled among those close to Pepita about volatile episodes, suggesting a dark undercurrent of domestic abuse and Nick's battle with alcoholism. Although these allegations were unconfirmed, the collective concern of her friends and family hinted at a disturbing possibility.

On March 24th, 2020, Pepita and her mother Anita, who shared a deep connection, spent a typical day together, laughing and talking over McDonald's. That evening, Anita dropped Pepita at Nick's house in South Albuquerque. With a smile and a heartfelt "Thanks, Mom. I love you," Pepita exited the car, unbeknownst to Anita, these were the final words she would hear from her daughter.

In the subsequent days, Anita's attempts to reach Pepita were met with unsettling silence. Alarm escalated on March 27th when she contacted Nick and learned he was also unaware of Pepita's whereabouts. Nick described their last night together: an evening out, an argument, and Pepita leaving abruptly. He hadn't seen her since that night.

Anita's heart sank with a foreboding sense of dread. On March 28th, 2020, filled with unease, she contacted the Albuquerque police to report Pepita missing. Yet, her pleas hit a wall of protocol; since Pepita was an adult, she was within her rights to disappear. The Navajo police, constrained by jurisdictional limits, echoed a similar stance. Anita was engulfed by a profound sense of solitude in her quest.

Yet, she wasn't alone in her pursuit. Shelda, Pepita's sister, stood steadfastly by her side. They reached out to the local media, seeking to highlight Pepita's story and share her missing person flyer. But their attempts faced resistance, and their appeals were often turned down.

In a confusing twist, Nick mentioned receiving a text from Pepita after she left, in which she claimed to be leaving him for another man, possibly someone they encountered on the night of their argument. However, the identity of these men remained unknown, deepening the enigma of Pepita's disappearance.

Compounding their plight was the emergence of the COVID-19 pandemic in March 2020. This global upheaval hindered Anita and Shelda's efforts to find Pepita. The pandemic's grip on the world transformed bustling streets into ghost towns, dampening the effectiveness of their flyer distribution and leaving Pepita's whereabouts veiled in mystery.

As COVID-19 dominated news cycles, Pepita's disappearance on March 24th, 2020, struggled to capture attention. This crisis, engulfing the globe, pushed her case into the shadows, tragically coinciding with her disappearance. Her family's search for answers, amidst a world in chaos, felt ignored and fruitless, a desperate quest overshadowed by a global emergency.

In the eerie quiet that followed Pepita's vanishing, Anita's world stood still until a message arrived from Pepita's number on March 30th, 2020. Her heart fluttered with a fragile mix of hope and fear. Could this be Pepita? But the text shattered those hopes; the sender was a stranger who claimed to have bought the phone on the street. Questions swirled in the air: Who sold Pepita's phone? Could this clue lead to her whereabouts? Yet answers remained elusive, and the trail seemed to grow colder by the minute.

Nick's response to the situation drew scrutiny. He didn't report Pepita missing until April 19, 2020, nearly a month after her disappearance. This delay was puzzling, stirring speculation about his thoughts and motives during that time. Was he influenced by pressure from Pepita's family, or did he think his involvement might accelerate the investigation? His late reaction only deepened the mystery surrounding Pepita's case.

Time marched on, but Anita and Shelda's resolve to find Pepita grew stronger. They became advocates for a cause greater than their own grief: the plight of missing and murdered indigenous women. Their activism took them to marches, protests, and awareness campaigns, transforming their sorrow into a crusade for justice, not just for Pepita but for all indigenous women facing similar fates.

The location of Pepita's last sighting added layers of complexity to the case. Albuquerque, New Mexico, a stark contrast to the reservation and an hour's drive away, brought jurisdictional hurdles and challenges unique to its urban setting. These factors complicated the investigation, making the task of finding Pepita and unraveling the truth behind her disappearance an even more daunting endeavor.

In the shadow of a global health crisis, the mission to find Pepita unfolded against Albuquerque's urban canvas. Anita and Shelda, armed with a blend of hope, unwavering resolve, and the weight of sorrow, continued their relentless pursuit of the truth.

Albuquerque, the largest city in New Mexico, is a bustling urban hub nestled in a contrasting landscape. Surrounded by arid deserts, towering mountains, and the meandering Rio Grande, the city's dynamic terrain underscores the daunting task of searching for a missing person. Pepita's vanishing, a poignant reminder of the complexities involved in urban search operations, especially for indigenous individuals, stands out in this diverse environment.

The city's demographic makeup, with a small Native American population, starkly contrasts the composition of nearby reservations. This disparity highlights potential issues in the city's approach to cases involving indigenous persons, such as Pepita's. Classified as an MMIW (Missing and Murdered Indigenous Women) case, her disappearance raises crucial questions about the commitment and resources dedicated by local authorities in the search.

The Navajo Nation, Pepita's homeland, is a vast territory, the largest reservation in the United States by area. Spanning over 27,000 square miles and comprising 17 million acres, it is governed by its elected president and vice president. They work alongside the U.S. Bureau of Indian Affairs, managing the intricate relationship between tribal and federal jurisdictions. However, the reservation faces significant hurdles: constrained resources, limited job prospects, high poverty levels, and a resultant higher crime rate. These challenges intensify the MMIW crisis within the community, making cases like Pepita's all the more distressing and complex.

In the summer of 2022, a pivotal moment unfolded as the FBI initiated a partnership with the Navajo Nation to tackle the escalating issue of missing indigenous persons. This alliance represented a significant stride in heightening awareness and harnessing resources to unravel these cases. By October, an extensive database was launched, cataloging 192 missing individuals from the Navajo Nation, each entry echoing a story awaiting closure.

Time has marched on without any sign of Pepita, with speculation surrounding Nick, who, though not formally designated a suspect, is eyed with suspicion by many.

Various hypotheses circulate about Pepita's fate. Could she have embarked on a new journey with a newfound companion, or did she encounter a darker destiny? It seems improbable that she would intentionally cut off ties with her tight-knit family, plunging them into a vortex of unresolved queries and perpetual sorrow. The cityscape of Albuquerque, blending urban intricacies with the vast, untamed outskirts, reflects the intricate and profound nature of Pepita's case. It's a riddle set in a milieu of cultural, geographical, and societal juxtapositions, where the quest for answers perseveres amid the rhythm of urban life and the haunting stillness of the desert.

Jennifer Cahill Shadle

J ennifer Cahill, born on the frosty winter day of January 6, 1966, entered the world as a beacon of vibrancy and charisma. Her parents, Johanna and Ed, fondly recall their daughter's childhood, brimming with a zest for life and a magnetic personality. Jennifer's passions extended deeply into the realms of art and film, showcasing an innate creative spirit. Furthermore, she was conscientious about her physical well-being, often engaging in activities that reflected her commitment to health and fitness.

As Jennifer blossomed into a young woman, her path crossed with Sean Shadle. At that pivotal moment, Jennifer was still navigating the complexities of youth, yet she found herself irresistibly drawn to Sean's undeniable confidence, ambitious nature, and striking good looks. This encounter, however, was a turning point, observed keenly by her family. They noted a subtle shift in Jennifer's demeanor, a change they didn't perceive as entirely positive. Her self-esteem seemed to waver, and there were instances when family disputes arose, during which Jennifer would staunchly align with Sean, even at the expense of her own kin. These moments, though possibly trivial, might hold significance in the grander tapestry of her life's story.

At the tender age of 21, Jennifer and Sean solidified their bond through marriage. The young couple settled in State College, Pennsylvania, a bustling college town cradled in the heart of the state, known primarily as the home of Penn State University. Here, amidst a population of just over 42,000, they began to build their life together. Sean carved a notable niche for himself in the insurance industry, earning a mixed bag of admiration and disdain among the locals.

As time wore on, Jennifer faced her own battles, grappling with issues related to alcohol. Her journey toward recovery included joining Alcoholics Anonymous and seeking weekly therapy sessions, efforts that were met with encouraging progress. Unfortunately, Sean's support in her journey was less than ideal. On one notable occasion, he presented Jennifer with a bottle of alcohol to 'celebrate' her first year of sobriety, a gesture that was as perplexing as it was hurtful.

In 2013, after nearly three decades of marriage, the couple's journey took a sharp turn as Sean initiated divorce proceedings. Initially, Jennifer resisted, the weight of this decision bearing heavily on her. Eventually, the stress became too much, and she retreated to the comforting embrace of her mother's home in Orwigsburg, Pennsylvania, a quaint town nestled a considerable distance from State College.

This new chapter saw Jennifer taking up a position at a local insurance agency, a semblance of independence in the wake of her tumultuous marriage. However, the distance from her three children proved too great a burden, and she soon found herself drawn back to State College. Without a car, she relied on the generosity of friends and the affordability of modest hotels while she sought to rebuild her life, brick by brick.

Amidst the final stages of the divorce, a glimmer of hope emerged. The court decreed that Sean was to provide Jennifer with a substantial monthly spousal support, a financial lifeline that promised a fresh start. Emboldened by this development, Jennifer began to scout for apartments, her spirits lifting as she envisioned a future filled with newfound independence and financial stability.

On the seemingly ordinary day of May 15, 2014, Jennifer Cahill set out to tackle a list of errands, her steps echoing the routine of everyday life. At this time, Jennifer had found temporary refuge in the familiar surroundings of a local hotel in State College. Her accommodations varied between two establishments – the Roadway Inn and the Quality Inn – each offering a haven during a tumultuous period in her life. With no vehicle at her disposal, Jennifer navigated her way through the town either by hailing taxis or embracing the simplicity of walking.

That afternoon, amidst her errands, Jennifer took a moment to connect with her family over the phone. During the call, her voice carried a note of optimism as she shared her plans and aspirations for the future. She spoke of her earnest efforts in securing a place of her own, a sanctuary where she could turn the page and start anew. There was a palpable sense of hope in her words, indicating that this day was shaping up to be a positive one for Jennifer.

However, the following day cast a shadow of worry and uncertainty. Jennifer's mother, Johanna, found herself unable to reach her daughter. It became apparent that Jennifer had misplaced her cell phone, severing an important lifeline of communication. As the hours stretched into a full day without any contact, Johanna's concern deepened, transforming into a gnawing sense of dread.

By the time another day had slipped by with no word from Jennifer, Johanna's worry escalated to full-blown alarm. She reached out to Jennifer's eldest daughter, seeking any clue that might shed light on her whereabouts, but to no avail – she, too, had not heard from Jennifer.

The situation took a more desperate turn by May 20th. With anxiety gripping her heart, Johanna plunged into action, contacting the local police in State College. State College, an intriguing tapestry of communities and neighborhoods, is officially designated as a borough in Pennsylvania. It is encompassed by several distinct areas, each with its own unique identity.

Jennifer had last been seen in the area of Ferguson, so it was to the Ferguson

Police that Johanna turned in her hour of need. She hoped for urgency, for immediate action, but the response from the Ferguson Police was disheart-eningly lackluster. Their apparent disinterest in the case added a frustrating and worrying obstacle to the already distressing situation.

Jennifer Cahill, at the age of 48, was a woman who had earned the right to make her own choices, independent and free from the need to justify her actions to anyone. Amidst the whirlwind of a stressful period in her life, Jennifer's sudden disappearance raised a myriad of questions. The speculation was rife – some thought she might have sought solace in a getaway, an escape from the tumultuous events unfolding around her.

When the police inquired Sean, Jennifer's estranged husband, about her potential whereabouts, his response was nonchalant at best. He suggested, with a casual shrug, that Jennifer might have sought refuge in a rehabilitation facility. This conjecture, however, was met with skepticism from Jennifer's family. They argued that it was implausible for Jennifer to check into rehab without informing them. Given her close relationship with her mother, Daley, and her daughters, whom she conversed with daily, her family found it hard to believe that she would embark on such a significant step without a word.

The police, however, showed a reluctance to delve deeper into the matter. Considering Jennifer's adult status and the lack of apparent urgency, they were disinclined to pursue an investigation. This lack of interest was further compounded by Sean's stature in the community – a well-known and influential figure, whose words seemed to carry weight with the local law enforcement.

Frustrated and desperate for answers, Jennifer's family turned to social media and contacted investigators, determined to uncover the truth. The circumstances surrounding her disappearance, coinciding with a contentious divorce and a recent court order requiring Sean to pay her a substantial sum, raised suspicions. While Sean had his defenders, there were also those who doubted his innocence. Even his own sister came forward, expressing her belief that Sean might be withholding crucial information and questioning his integrity.

A breakthrough, or so it seemed, came when surveillance footage from a Walmart on North Atherton Street in Ferguson, State College, was scrutinized. Captured on camera at 4:51 PM on May 15th, Jennifer was seen leaving the store, alone. This development begged several questions: What led the investigators to check this specific footage, and how did they pinpoint the exact day and time? It seemed plausible that someone might have reported seeing Jennifer there, or the timeline could have been deduced from her last known contact with her family earlier that day.

The search for Jennifer began to gain momentum, although she was not yet officially listed as a missing person in the system. The investigators were hesitant to escalate the case to that level. Curiously, while Jennifer was last seen at Walmart, reports indicated that she was without her phone or wallet. The loss of her phone had been previously noted, but the absence of her wallet added another layer of mystery. Was it lost along with her phone?

Further intrigue was added when it was revealed that Jennifer had used a phone at the Walmart customer service desk, likely due to her lack of a personal cell phone. Surprisingly, no one thought to interview the clerk who interacted with her. As of this point, that clerk remained unqueried about their encounter with Jennifer.

Additional information surfaced later, suggesting that Jennifer had also lost her credit card, and arrangements were supposedly being made by her daughter and ex-husband to provide her with a replacement.

In June, a full month after her disappearance, the police finally took the critical step of entering Jennifer Cahill Shadle into their missing person database, a move that marked a shift in the urgency of the case. Meanwhile, Jennifer's family, grappling with unanswered questions and growing anxiety, visited the hotel where she had been staying. They were informed by the hotel staff that attempts to reach Sean, Jennifer's estranged husband, had been in vain. The room, which had been left seemingly abandoned, was a silent witness to the mysterious circumstances surrounding Jennifer's disappearance. Sean, it seemed, had been neglecting the calls from the hotel about Jennifer's belongings.

Amidst the growing concern, voices began to emerge, shedding light on Sean's character. There were claims of abuse, and many speculated about his possible motives for making Jennifer vanish. The timing of Jennifer's disappearance was particularly suspicious. Sean had recently been ordered to make substantial spousal support payments, a financial burden that he reportedly resented. Despite this, Jennifer and Sean's children resided with him and staunchly supported their father.

The investigation saw Sean brought in for questioning, where he was subjected to a lie detector test. The results, however, were deemed inconclusive. There were whispers among Jennifer's family members and friends that Sean may have manipulated the test's outcome by consuming marijuana prior to the examination. The veracity of these claims remained unverified, and questions arose as to why a retest wasn't conducted if such suspicions existed.

Further intensifying the mystery, trained cadaver and human remains detection dogs were deployed to search Sean's home and property. Yet, despite the thorough search, nothing incriminating was found. Externally, while the situation appeared damning for Sean, there was a glaring absence of concrete evidence linking him to Jennifer's disappearance.

As months passed with little progress, Jennifer's family, frustrated by the lack of substantial response from local law enforcement, decided to hire a private investigator. This decision proved pivotal as the investigator uncovered new leads. Previously, the last confirmed sighting of Jennifer had been the

Walmart surveillance footage at 4:51 PM on May 15, 2014. However, the private investigator revealed that Jennifer was also spotted a few hours later at a tanning salon and then at the Don Patron Mexican restaurant, both located in the same shopping plaza.

These findings were relayed to law enforcement by the family. Meanwhile, Sean and the children remained away from the media spotlight during the ongoing investigation. A family member managed to speak with Jennifer and Sean's daughter, who revealed knowledge of her mother's sightings at the salon and restaurant. However, they had chosen not to report this information to the police, deeming it insignificant.

The case resembled one covered previously, marked by a significant divide among family members. This rift was evident on a Facebook page created by Jennifer's family, where arguments and discussions among family members, friends, and community members were frequent. There were two distinct factions, each with their own perspectives on the situation.

A year after Jennifer's disappearance, the family advocated for FBI involvement, believing that the federal agency could bring new resources and a fresh approach to the case. However, the local police resisted this suggestion, maintaining that they were handling the case to the best of their abilities. A family member directly appealed to Diana Conrad, the Chief of Police for the Ferguson department, requesting FBI involvement. The response from Chief Conrad, as reported in the Happy Valley Citizen blog, acknowledged the ongoing investigation but provided little satisfaction to the family, who continued to feel ignored and disrespected by the police. Some believed that this treatment was influenced by the department's close relationship with Sean.

Approximately a year after her disappearance, a peculiar development emerged. Sean reported that someone had attempted to file health insurance claims under Jennifer's name, suggesting to some that she might still be alive. However, there was no activity on her social security number, bank accounts, or any other indicators to corroborate this theory. The family urged the authorities to investigate these claims, suspecting either a fraud attempt or Jennifer's involvement, but the police declined further inquiry. Frustrated, the family hired another private investigator, who traced the IP address of the claim to New Jersey, but could not unearth any additional information.

The numerous leads and discoveries made by private investigators, all funded by the family, highlighted the growing desperation and determination to uncover the truth. Amidst these developments, Sean maintained his stance that Jennifer was alive, possibly living elsewhere. However, some speculated that Sean, with his insurance expertise, might have orchestrated these leads as a diversion, further complicating an already baffling and heart-wrenching case.

Christian Ferguson

C hristian Ferguson's journey began on a crisp autumn day, October 9th, 1993, in the vibrant city of St. Louis, Missouri. Nestled along the majestic western bank of the Mississippi River, St. Louis is not just a city, but the heart of a sprawling metropolitan area, home to over three million souls. The city, known for its iconic Gateway Arch, stands as a historical monument, marking St. Louis as the "Gateway to the West."

Into this lively urban tapestry, Christian was born to Dawan and Theda, marking the beginning of a story that intertwines joy, adversity, and the resilience of the human spirit. From the moment he nestled in his mother's arms, Christian was the epitome of a healthy newborn, bringing joy and hope to his family.

However, just as Theda prepared to leave the hospital with her bundle of joy, their lives took a dramatic and unforeseen turn. In the early hours of a seemingly ordinary day, Christian's health plummeted, catapulting the family into a whirlwind of fear and uncertainty. Rushed to the Cardinal Glennon Children's Medical Center by medevac, Christian's condition baffled the medical experts. A healthy baby boy was now fighting for his life, leaving his family and doctors in a state of bewildered distress.

After extensive testing, the medical mystery unraveled, revealing a rare and life-threatening genetic condition: citrullinemia, a disorder that impairs the body's ability to process nitrogen, causing harmful substances to accumulate in the bloodstream. This rare urea cycle disorder affects roughly one in 57,000 children and comes in two types. Christian's case was of the more severe type 1, appearing shortly after birth and posing immediate and serious risks.

For three agonizing days, Christian lay in a coma, his family clinging to hope. The diagnosis, while devastating, brought some clarity and opened the path for treatment. The family faced a challenging road ahead, involving a strict regimen of medications and dietary restrictions. Theda, determined and resourceful, devised her own methods to administer the medication, easing the process for young Christian.

As Christian's condition stabilized, Theda and Dawan brought him home, marking the beginning of a new chapter. Their unwed relationship, beginning in their high school years, now took a significant turn. Theda, deeply in love with Dawan and influenced by her Catholic upbringing, longed for marriage, hoping to provide a stable and traditional family for their children. Despite Dawan's initial hesitation, the couple married on Valentine's Day in 1994, just months after Christian's birth, and soon welcomed a second child, Connor.

Yet, as Christian grew, the fragile harmony within the family began to unravel. Dawan and Theda's relationship, strained by the pressures of parenting a child with a severe medical condition and their own personal differences, deteriorated. Despite the love that once brought them together, the couple found themselves embroiled in escalating conflicts, ultimately leading to physical altercations and heartbreak.

The situation reached a breaking point when Theda, following a particularly intense dispute, left with both children to seek refuge with her parents. Dawan, responding with a swift legal action, filed for divorce and sought full custody of Christian and Connor, igniting a contentious battle that would have lasting implications for everyone involved.

In the wake of their tumultuous annulment in 1998, Theda and Dawan found themselves entangled in a complex legal labyrinth, each fiercely battling for the custody of their children. The annulment, catalyzed by a technical mishap in their marriage license, left Theda with full custody initially, but this arrangement was soon to be contested in a dramatic turn of events.

Within just a month, the ex-couple were back in the courtroom, each armed with accusations against the other. Dawan's grievances centered around Theda's alleged non-compliance with the visitation agreement and her refusal to provide Christian's essential medications. Theda, in her defense, brought forth concerns about Dawan's legal troubles regarding traffic violations and his alleged neglect of Christian's health needs during his custody periods. This acrimonious battle, filled with vehement exchanges, led to a significant shift in custody arrangements.

A court-appointed guardian ad litem, after evaluating the situation, sided with Dawan, influencing the judge's decision. This resulted in Dawan being granted temporary custody until a new trial. Theda, determined to prove her dedication to her children's well-being, organized protests outside the courthouse, gathering support from friends and family.

The proceedings were further complicated by disparities in financial stability and legal representation. Dawan, employed by his stepfather's company, had access to a high-priced lawyer funded by his stepfather, while Theda struggled on a minimum wage income. In 1999, Judge Thomas Frawley's final ruling landed heavily in Dawan's favor, granting him full custody and ordering Theda to pay child support, a crushing blow for her as she was granted limited visitation rights.

Despite the legal turbulence, Christian seemed to be faring well, attending school and managing his illness. However, in January 2001, tragedy struck. Christian was found unconscious and rushed to the hospital, where he suffered a severe seizure and lapsed into a coma. This medical emergency sparked a fiery confrontation between Theda and Dawan at the hospital, escalating to the point where both sought to restrict the other's hospital visitation rights.

The hospital incident led to a court order splitting visitation times, ensuring the parents wouldn't cross paths. Theda, not one to retreat silently, accused Dawan of neglecting Christian's medical needs. Christian's doctor, however, defended Dawan, stating that he had responded appropriately under the circumstances. Nonetheless, there were past incidents where Dawan reportedly hadn't administered Christian's medication, fueling Theda's concerns.

Unwavering in her fight, Theda took her protest to the hospital and contacted the local police's child abuse unit to investigate Dawan, though no substantial evidence was found to warrant a full investigation. Christian emerged from his coma in February, but the ordeal had left him with significant brain damage, unable to speak, walk, or eat without assistance.

After a grueling six months in the hospital, Christian returned to Dawan's care. Remarkably, in the following year, the icy relations between Theda and Dawan began to thaw. Dawan allowed Theda increased visitation and even relied on her for help with the boys on occasion.

In 2003, the saga took another twist when the Department of Health and Services, citing Christian's non-enrollment in school, canceled Dawan's nursing benefits, crucial for Christian's care at home. Theda, during a weekend visit, noticed concerning signs of neglect and rushed Christian to the hospital. As tensions escalated, Theda found herself once again in court, fighting for custody of her sons.

The saga of Christian Ferguson's disappearance took a pivotal turn when both parents, Theda and Dawan, once again stood before Judge Frawley. The atmosphere in the courtroom was charged with tension as Dawan faced the possibility of being held in contempt for not adhering to the court-ordered visitation schedule. The judge reiterated the importance of abiding by the court's decisions and ordered the resumption of visitation on June 14, 2003.

However, a heart-wrenching twist in the tale was about to unfold, as Theda would tragically never see her son again.

On the fateful morning of June 11th, just days before the scheduled visitation, Dawan reported a harrowing incident. He claimed that he was taking Christian, then nine years old and suffering from his illness, to the hospital after a night of severe vomiting. In a rush, Dawan said he wrapped Christian, clad only in a diaper, in a blanket and placed him in the backseat of his maroon 1998 Ford Expedition SUV, embarking on a journey that would soon turn into a nightmare.

Shortly after 6:00 a.m., the St. Louis Police Department received a frantic 911 call from Dawan. He reported that his SUV, with Christian still inside, had been stolen. Dawan recounted that he had parked and left his vehicle running with the keys in the ignition while he used a payphone to call the hospital. This critical moment of leaving the car unattended, he claimed, was when the vehicle, along with his ill son, was taken.

As Dawan relayed these events to the arriving officers, he emphasized the direness of Christian's situation due to his medical condition, explaining that without timely treatment, his son's life was in grave danger. The police immediately launched an extensive search operation, issuing an all-points bulletin for Dawan's vehicle and an Amber Alert for Christian. The search was a race against time, as medical staff warned that Christian's survival without his medication was perilously limited.

The story swiftly captured media attention, with broadcasts and alerts disseminating information about the alleged abduction. Theda learned of her son's disappearance through the television news, a revelation that left her in a state of shock and growing suspicion.

While the community rallied in the search, a crucial development occurred within two hours of Dawan's report. A resident on Ron Barr Lane alerted the Ferguson Police Department to an abandoned SUV at the end of a cul-de-sac. Officer Charles Creely responded and identified the vehicle as Dawan's. However, the relief of finding the SUV was overshadowed by the alarming absence of Christian. The vehicle, found unlocked with the keys still in the ignition, offered no clue to Christian's whereabouts.

Investigators combed the area, using dogs to track Christian's scent and extending the search to the nearby woods and train tracks, but no trace of the boy was found. Meanwhile, detectives examining the SUV encountered puzzling inconsistencies. Despite being reported stolen, the vehicle was abandoned only five miles from the payphone Dawan had used, and it contained numerous valuable items, including a laptop, two cellphones, binoculars, a bulletproof vest, and a digital camera. This raised questions about the thief's motives and actions.

Further complicating the narrative, Dawan, who worked as a bounty hunter, had two functioning cell phones in the SUV. This contradicted his claim of needing to use a payphone to contact the hospital. Additionally, records showed no call to the Children's Medical Center from the payphone Dawan claimed to have used.

When the vehicle was towed for further examination, Dawan was taken to the scene and questioned in greater detail. His cooperation waned when he was asked to take a polygraph test, which he declined, subsequently requesting an attorney and ceasing his cooperation with the investigation. Dawan's attorney, John Rogers, maintained this stance despite ongoing requests for assistance from law enforcement.

Monica, Dawan's wife, recounted to detectives that on the night before Christian's disappearance, Dawan, working late as a bounty hunter, had returned home at some point during the night. She was only made aware of the dire situation with Christian around 6:00 a.m. when Dawan called to inform her of the SUV theft and Christian's presence in the stolen vehicle.

Monica's account to the officers included a harrowing recollection of a previous hospitalization of Christian that had resulted in a coma, leaving him severely mentally handicapped, to the point where she described him as unable to communicate and in a vegetative state.

Monica admitted that she was not involved in Christian's care, citing the complexity of administering his medications and the specialized care he required, which Dawan primarily provided, including changing his diapers. This added another layer of complexity to the case, as it indicated Dawan's central role in Christian's daily care.

Further intriguing insights were provided by Monica's daughter, Deshaun, who reported waking up around 4:00 a.m. and hearing the SUV start up and leave the house, though she did not witness Dawan or Christian at that time. Christian's younger brother, Connor, also shared his observation of Dawan entering their shared room, wrapping Christian in a blanket, and taking him out to the SUV under the cover of darkness.

Investigators faced a conundrum as they pieced together the timeline of events. The official weather report indicated that sunrise on that day was at 5:36 a.m., with early twilight at 5:04 a.m. This raised questions about the timing of Dawan's actions and his call to 911 at 6:09 a.m., especially considering the relatively short distance from their home to the payphone he allegedly used.

A search of the residence revealed a neatly made bed in Christian and Connor's room, with a heavy smell of urine and soiled clothing, including blue pajama bottoms that Connor mentioned Christian had kicked off during the night. This added to the growing suspicion about the events leading up to Christian's disappearance.

Monica consented to a search of their residence, where officers found more evidence of Christian's living conditions. They discovered his clothing, soiled and in disarray, and a bed that reeked of urine. The details painted a picture of neglect and raised serious concerns about the care Christian was receiving at home.

Intriguingly, when Monica was questioned about their connections in Ferguson, she mentioned a friend, Lakeisha Mays. Detectives visiting Mays found her gold 1998 Chevrolet Malibu sedan missing, and upon its later discovery near the payphone Dawan claimed to use, the plot thickened. Mays initially downplayed her relationship with Dawan and Monica, but under further questioning, she admitted to a complex, intertwined sexual relationship with the couple.

Ozell Scott, a fellow bounty hunter and associate of Dawan, shed light on the events of the night before Christian's disappearance. He observed bags of clothing in Dawan's SUV, which Dawan explained belonged to Mays. Scott also recalled overhearing phone arguments between Dawan, Monica, and Mays, suggesting a fraught dynamic in their relationships.

The investigation uncovered a letter, purportedly written by Monica, detailing an ongoing sexual relationship involving Dawan, Monica, and Mays. This discovery added yet another layer of complexity to the case, hinting at potential motives and entanglements that might have influenced the events leading up to Christian's disappearance.

Margaret Binion, a nurse assigned to provide home care for Christian, shared disturbing observations. She noticed signs of potential physical abuse and neglect, including instances where Christian was left home alone and in soiled clothing. Her experiences, along with reports from other nurses, painted a grim picture of Christian's home life, marked by inadequate care and a lack of attention to his medical needs.

As the investigation continued, no significant leads or evidence leading to Christian's whereabouts emerged. Eight weeks after his reported disappearance, the St. Louis Police Department publicly expressed their belief that Christian was deceased, though the case remained open as a missing person's investigation.

Nurses who had been involved in Christian's care from 2001 to 2002 recounted numerous instances of neglect and abuse, painting a harrowing picture of his living conditions. Over five nurses reported situations where critical necessities, like timely diaper changes, were often delayed or overlooked by Dawan, causing discomfort and distress to Christian.

In one alarming incident, a nurse quit her job after a confrontation with Dawan. She had been berated by him for not ordering new diapers, a task that was, in fact, Dawan's responsibility. His aggressive response left her feeling intimidated and fearful.

The situation regarding Christian's medication was equally concerning. Pharmacy records revealed a disturbing pattern of negligence in refilling essential medications for Christian. For instance, sodium benzoate, crucial for managing his urea cycle disorder, was not refilled for 74 days, far exceeding the prescribed 30-day supply. This lapse in medication was not an isolated incident but a recurring problem across several of Christian's prescriptions. The most egregious example involved a solution called Polycitra, which was not refilled for a staggering 141 days.

Dr. Grange, a clinical geneticist who followed Christian's health since his birth, noted a concerning trend. When nurses were responsible for Christian's care, he rarely needed hospitalization. However, in their absence, hospitalizations became more frequent, suggesting that proper care at home was not being administered. During her last consultation with Christian in March 2003, nurse Kimberly Nero expressed dietary concerns, indicating that Christian hadn't been seen by Dr. Grange for an entire year, despite the recommendation for quarterly check-ups.

In the midst of this, Christian's younger brother Connor shared his observations, which were deeply troubling. He described Christian as having become very thin, to the point where his bones were visible. Connor would sneak food to Christian, noting his brother's constant hunger. Connor also recounted a particularly distressing incident shortly before Christian went missing. He found Christian extremely sick, lying flat on his back with his eyes rolled back, and the feeding tube (referred to as the 'G button' by Connor) missing.

The theory investigators formed was chilling. They hypothesized that Dawan had returned home around 4:00 a.m., removed Christian, who was already deceased, and disposed of his body at an undisclosed location. Dawan then allegedly abandoned his SUV, used Lakeisha Mays' vehicle to travel to the payphone, and reported Christian as missing.

In response to these alarming circumstances, Christian's younger brother Connor was temporarily placed in the custody of his grandparents, with a permanent custody hearing scheduled. Despite Theda's efforts and the judge sealing the court file, custody was ultimately awarded to Dawan's mother and stepfather. Theda's allegations of abuse and neglect couldn't be substantiated in the eyes of the court, leaving many questions unanswered.

Connor's living situation with his grandparents was stable initially, but by 2007, difficulties arose, leading to him being placed in Theda's care under specific conditions, including not speaking to the media about Christian's disappearance.

Theda, relentless in her pursuit of justice, founded "Looking for an Angel," a nonprofit dedicated to supporting families of missing relatives. She has been instrumental in keeping Christian's story alive, organizing various events to raise awareness and funds. Her determination is unwavering, as she vows to continue her fight until justice is served for her son.

Meanwhile, law enforcement officials, despite their suspicions and beliefs, expressed their frustration with the limitations of the evidence at hand. Off-the-record, they acknowledged their belief in Dawan's guilt but were wary of pursuing a trial without sufficient evidence to avoid the risk of double jeopardy.

As the years passed, Theda's grief transformed into a force for change, as she tirelessly worked to support others facing similar tragedies. Her organization, Looking for an Angel, became a beacon of hope and assistance for families grappling with the anguish of having missing loved ones. Despite the passage of time, the mystery of Christian Ferguson's disappearance remains unsolved, a testament to the enduring heartache and unresolved questions that continue to haunt all those who cared for him.

Patty Vaughan

Patty Brightwell, born on a warm summer day on August 17, 1964, entered the world as the cherished daughter of Patsy Wallace and Billy Brightwell. Her childhood was painted with the vibrant hues of life in Okinawa, where she attended the bustling halls of Kuboski High School. It was here that Patty's journey began to take an exciting turn.

After her graduation, a chance encounter brought Jerry Ray Vaughan, affectionately known as JR, into her life. Their connection was instant and deep, blossoming into a love that led them down the aisle in the heart of San Antonio, Texas, in May 1985. Patty, a youthful 21, and JR embarked on a new chapter together, united in marriage.

The ensuing years saw Patty and JR dance through the rhythms of life, relocating to various places like Portland, Georgia, and Virginia. These moves were driven by JR's career in construction, a field demanding mobility and adaptability. Amidst these changes, Patty's life was further enriched by the arrival of three beautiful children: Brittany, their spirited daughter, and two sons, Ray and Kyle, each with their own unique charms. By 1996, they were bustling youngsters, aged nine, eight, and six, respectively, each a reflection of Patty's love and dedication.

In December 1990, the family found their anchor in Lavonia, Texas, a quaint town with a close-knit community, nestled about 25 miles east of San Antonio. Their home on Oak Park Road became a sanctuary, where Patty embraced the role of a stay-at-home mom, a decision made at JR's behest. Here, she cultivated a haven for her children, far from the impersonal environment of daycare.

Patty's spirit resonated with deep faith; she was a devout Christian, her soulful voice a staple in her church choir. Singing was more than a passion; it was a connection to her inner joy, a talent she had nurtured since her childhood. Her voice wasn't just melodious; it was a vessel of her profound love and faith.

Life in suburban Lavonia was picturesque. Patty, the epitome of a loving mother, devoted her entire being to her children. Their happiness was her world, and she went to great lengths to ensure they experienced a joyful childhood. Even her younger sister Jeannie, who spent time living with Patty and her family, fondly remembered Patty's nurturing nature, likening her to a second mother.

However, beneath this idyllic surface, there were undercurrents of strain in the Vaughan household. Over their 11-year marriage, JR's controlling demeanor cast a shadow over Patty's life. He insisted she remain at home, often subjected her to demeaning comments, and there were whispers of physical abuse, though never officially reported. Patty's family recalled incidents that hinted at this darker side, like JR's outburst involving a jar of mayo. Concerns grew as they noticed unexplained bruises on Patty.

Despite the outward appearance of a perfect suburban life, those closest to Patty knew of her growing unhappiness in the marriage. After she and JR separated, a transformation occurred. Patty's demeanor brightened considerably; she gained employment at Queenie Electric, a local company, rediscovering her independence.

During this newfound chapter, Patty rekindled a romance with an old flame, Gary. They had a history dating back to their teenage years, before her marriage to JR. Circumstances had pulled them apart back then, but now, with both free from their previous commitments, they reunited. Patty's family, though not well-acquainted with Gary, noticed her renewed happiness and wholeheartedly supported this blossoming relationship.

However, not everyone shared this supportive view. Patty, a devout Christian, faced criticism from her church community. A particularly painful incident occurred when a fellow churchgoer reported seeing her with Gary at a local Dairy Queen to the church minister. Despite both Patty and JR being separated, the minister publicly reprimanded her during choir practice, chastising her in front of her peers. This unjust treatment deeply hurt Patty, as her church and choir were integral parts of her life and identity.

In the midst of her personal tumult, Patty held her relationship with Gary close, not allowing external pressures to dim their growing bond. This blossomed beautifully on Christmas Eve when Patty invited Gary to join her family's dinner, marking his inaugural introduction to everyone. The evening was adorned with warmth and laughter, with Gary gifting Patty a heart-shaped pendant, symbolizing their affection. The night resonated with genuine camaraderie and joy, everyone embracing Gary as part of their circle.

However, the serenity of the evening was short-lived. Christmas Day was supposed to be a time of festive unity, with JR planning to visit the Oak Park Road home. The intention was to celebrate with their children, exchanging gifts and sharing a meal, all in an effort to maintain normalcy amidst their separation. Following this, Patty planned to bring the kids to her sister Kathy's for a grand family Christmas dinner. But fate had other plans.

Alarm bells rang when Patty failed to show up at the dinner. Concerned calls to her home were answered by JR, who claimed that Patty, engulfed in an argument, had left around 6:30 PM to meet Gary and had not returned. This was unlike Patty; abandoning her children on Christmas was unthinkable, and not informing her family was out of character. Her family suspected that Patty would have sought solace at the dinner, surrounded by family and her beloved children.

By December 26th, with still no word from Patty, her family's worry escalated. Contacting Gary revealed that he too was oblivious to her whereabouts. This deepened the mystery and concern, as it was clear something was amiss. Prompted by their growing unease, one of Patty's cousins approached the Bexar County Sheriff's Department to file a missing person's report. However, they were met with bureaucratic barriers; a report couldn't be filed until she had been missing for 72 hours.

That afternoon, a chilling discovery was made. Patty's 1991 light blue Dodge Caravan was found abandoned on the side of Texas State Highway Loop 1604, about 15 miles from her home and five miles from her workplace. It was her boss who stumbled upon the vehicle; he hadn't noticed it on his morning commute but saw it on his way back. Concerned by Patty's absence at work and now the discovery of her abandoned car, he immediately called 911.

Upon investigation, the car presented more questions than answers. The front left tire was flat, the engine warm, suggesting recent use. Strangely, the interior was unusually clean, a stark contrast to the typical clutter of a mother of three. The seats were shampooed, still damp, and water pooled in the cup holders. Notably absent were Patty's purse and keys. Inside, men's clothing was found, including a red jumpsuit with the initials "JM" - a puzzling clue with no immediate connection.

Forensic examination of the car brought to light concerning details. It had been thoroughly wiped down, erasing fingerprints, including Patty's. Yet, investigators did find a set of prints that had been overlooked, along with traces of blood in the backseat and on the sliding door.

The sequence of events on the day her car was found only deepened the enigma. Her boss, who had passed the same route in the morning without noticing the vehicle, stumbled upon it on his way home, suggesting an occurrence in broad daylight — a scenario that seemed implausible for an abduction.

The mystery deepened with the discovery of the car's flat tire, which upon closer examination, bore no signs of puncture or damage, indicating it had been deliberately deflated. This was confirmed when tests revealed the tire could still hold air, undermining the theory of a random roadside breakdown. The cap had been removed, air released, and then meticulously replaced, an act of staging designed to mislead.

Moreover, the lack of struggle at the scene raised questions. Patty was known for her resilience and spirit, traits that would have prompted a fierce resistance in the face of danger. The absence of disturbed dirt, drag marks, or any indication of a scuffle contradicted the theory of a roadside abduction.

Adding to the web of confusion was the state of the van's interior. The driver's seat was pushed far back, not aligned with Patty's usual driving position. This, coupled with the mysteriously shampooed interior, traces of blood, and the absence of Patty's personal effects, suggested a calculated attempt to erase evidence and craft a deceptive narrative.

In light of these baffling clues, the investigation intensified. The police waived the 72-hour waiting period, and a massive search ensued, involving over 500 volunteers, friends, family, and law enforcement officers. Despite their fervent efforts, no significant leads were uncovered.

Gary, Patty's boyfriend, emerged as a cooperative and devastated figure in the midst of this crisis. Voluntarily approaching the police, submitting to a polygraph test, and actively participating in the searches, he demonstrated a commitment to finding Patty. Though he was relatively unknown to Patty's family prior to this ordeal, his unwavering support during the searches fostered a deeper connection with them. His solid alibi for Christmas Day and his tragic, unrelated death a few years later absolved him of suspicion.

Investigations also led to intriguing insights from Patty's close circles. A conversation with one of her sisters on Christmas morning hinted at emotional distress, revealing that Patty and JR had been arguing, an altercation audible in the background. JR's interaction with his sister Marilyn, where he portrayed Patty as unwell and requested her to take the children, suggested an attempt to isolate Patty.

JR's narrative of the events was one of marital discord, citing conflicts over Gary as the catalyst. He claimed that following their altercation, Patty left to see Gary at 6:30 PM, and that was the last he saw of her. However, peculiarities in JR's behavior post-disappearance raised eyebrows. His lack of involvement in the search efforts, under the guise of caring for the children, his apparent indifference to distributing missing person flyers, and his abrupt decision to break his apartment lease just days before Patty's disappearance were all elements that cast a shadow of doubt.

Furthermore, JR's actions in the immediate aftermath were unsettling. After ostensibly reconciling with Patty on Christmas Day and moving back into the family home, he filed for divorce the day after her disappearance. This action, juxtaposed with the mysterious circumstances, painted a picture of complex motivations and unresolved marital tensions.

On one hand, his claim that Patty stormed out to see Gary, never to return, seemed plausible in the heat of a marital dispute. But the sequence of his actions following this event painted a picture of a man either indifferent or calculatingly evasive. His haste in filing for divorce the day after Patty's disappearance, his attempt to break his apartment lease two days before she went missing, and his openness about their arguments concerning Gary were all actions that, rather than dispelling suspicion, seemed to intensify it.

Moreover, JR's lack of participation in the search efforts for Patty was striking. One might expect that, regardless of personal feelings, an 11-year partnership and shared parenthood would compel a degree of concern and involvement, yet this was conspicuously absent in JR's behavior. Adding to the aura of suspicion, JR swiftly replaced Patty's voice on their home answering machine with his own, a move that seemed to erase her presence prematurely.

In stark contrast to Gary's cooperative stance with the police, JR took a defensive approach. He refused a polygraph test, lawyered up, and declined any form of DNA or fingerprint testing that could have aided in either incriminating or exonerating him. He even went to the extent of preventing the police from speaking to their children or using their DNA samples, further hindering the investigation.

JR's control extended beyond his immediate family; his sister Marilyn played a protective role during the police search of their home. Her confrontational demeanor with investigators to the point of being escorted off the property suggested a defensive, possibly complicit stance.

The police's discovery of blood traces in various parts of the house, including the master bedroom and bathroom, escalated the case's gravity. Yet, surprisingly, the house wasn't sealed as a crime scene, allowing JR and the children to continue living there, potentially compromising evidence.

The DNA tests on the blood found both in Patty's car and the house confirmed it was hers, deepening the mystery and pointing to a grim possibility of foul play. The stagnation of the investigation led to extreme measures; in a desperate act, Patty's mother was arrested for assaulting JR with a baseball bat, indicative of the family's conviction of his involvement and frustration with the lack of progress in the case.

JR's subsequent actions did nothing to alleviate the suspicions. He gained custody of their children and cut off their contact with Patty's family. Meanwhile, rumors in the small town led to searches in various locations connected to JR, including a construction site he supervised and a property in Pleasanton, but these turned up no conclusive evidence.

In a twist, new DNA testing revealed female DNA in Patty's van that didn't match anyone in her family, pointing to the possibility of an unknown woman's involvement. Speculations arose about JR's sister's possible involvement, especially considering her behavior during the investigation.

The motive behind Patty's disappearance remained a puzzle. Jealousy over her new relationship, a desire for sole custody of the children, or other unknown factors could have played a role. Patty's family believed she was murdered at home and her body moved, with her car strategically abandoned to mislead investigators.

Over the years, JR's life moved on — he relocated several times, remarried, and even changed his name, but he kept Patty's children isolated from her family. The agony for Patty's family was twofold: the loss of Patty and the estrangement from her children. As Patty's sister Janine poignantly expressed, their longing transcended the need for justice; it was a deep yearning to find closure and lay Patty to rest. The case, shrouded in mystery and marred by frustration, left a haunting legacy of unanswered questions and a family torn apart by tragedy and uncertainty.

Bianca Piper

At just 13 years old, Bianca Piper lived in the small, serene town of Foley, Missouri. Outwardly, she appeared as a typical teenager filled with youthful energy. However, Bianca's life was anything but ordinary due to her struggles with ADHD and bipolar disorder, challenges that belied her young age. Her cognitive functioning was thought by some to be more akin to a much younger child, contrasting sharply with her actual age.

Managing her bipolar disorder was a daily battle, even with a rigorous medication schedule. The tumult of emotions and occasional outbursts, especially towards her mother, often overpowered the intended effects of her treatments.

On the evening of March 10, 2005, a simple argument erupted between Bianca and her mother, Shannon Tanner, over household chores. This minor dispute quickly escalated, with Bianca finding it difficult to control her intense feelings. Recalling a therapist's advice, Shannon considered a method they had previously used: taking a drive followed by a walk home to help Bianca calm down.

Given Bianca's young age, her mental health conditions, and developmental stage, this strategy might seem unusual. Nonetheless, driven by hope and perhaps desperation, Shannon opted to extend the walking distance that night. Instead of the half-mile they had previously tried, she drove Bianca a full mile away from their home, hoping the longer walk would aid in managing her daughter's mood.

However, as Shannon left Bianca to walk back alone at around 6:15 PM, there was a palpable sense of apprehension. The decision to let a young girl, grappling with such intricate mental health challenges, walk alone as dusk approached was fraught with worries and uncertainties.

As the evening light waned in Foley, Missouri, Shannon handed her daughter Bianca a flashlight, her emotions a blend of hope and concern. "Stay safe and don't talk to strangers. Come right back home," she advised, emphasizing the importance of safety around strangers. Shannon watched with a growing sense of unease as Bianca disappeared into the dimming light.

An hour passed, and Shannon's anxiety intensified. Bianca should have returned by now. Deciding to act, Shannon drove along the route where she'd left Bianca, expecting to find her on her way back, perhaps taking extra time to calm down. Arriving at the drop-off point, Shannon's heart dropped – there was no sign of Bianca.

Alarm took over. Shannon quickly sought the help of her boyfriend, and together they went from neighbor to neighbor, asking if anyone had spotted Bianca. Their search, however, yielded no results. Shannon's next step was to contact the police, where she felt the response lacked urgency. She firmly believed that all cases of missing children deserved immediate and serious attention.

As the night grew colder in Missouri, concerns for Bianca's wellbeing deepened. With temperatures plummeting, Bianca's light attire – just a sweatshirt and jeans – seemed dangerously inadequate. Fears mounted about her enduring the cold, the possibility of her getting lost, or encountering even graver dangers.

The next day, with Bianca still unaccounted for, the police initiated a full-scale search. A large team was deployed, including around a hundred officers, some on foot and others on horseback, complemented by aerial support from a helicopter. Checkpoints were set up, drivers were questioned, and volunteer firefighters joined in, meticulously searching each house, shed, and garage in the hope of finding any clue that would lead to Bianca.

Attention in the investigation shifted towards those close to Bianca, especially her mother, Shannon, and her boyfriend, Jim. As the last person to see Bianca, Shannon faced rigorous questioning and a cloud of suspicion. She recalled seeing another car on the road that night but could not provide specific details, a fact that offered little assistance. For Shannon, the reality of such a horrifying event occurring in her perceived safe community was unthinkable.

Suspicion naturally fell on Shannon, evoking mixed reactions in the community. While some of this scrutiny might be seen as warranted given the situation, it also raised questions about the role and accountability of professional advice in sensitive matters. Shannon had acted on a therapist's recommendation, highlighting a critical point about the appropriateness of advice from professionals in varying contexts.

Given Bianca's age, her ADHD and bipolar disorder diagnosis, and her reportedly younger mental age, allowing her to walk alone in the dark raised significant concerns. Alternative measures, such as accompanying her on the walk or maintaining a safe following distance by car, might have been more prudent options. The vulnerability of young teenagers, especially those with mental health challenges, walking alone at night is a concern that becomes more acute against the backdrop of numerous cases illustrating the risks involved.

Intriguingly, both Shannon and Jim passed polygraph tests. However, the reliability of such tests is widely debated and they are not considered legally conclusive. Passing a polygraph test does not confirm innocence, just as failing does not prove guilt. This aspect of the investigation underscores the complexities and limitations in using polygraph tests as definitive evidence in serious cases like missing children.

During a media briefing, Shannon, alongside Bianca's biological father, David Piper, offered more details about Bianca's past. She had been in therapy from a young age and was taking medication to manage aggressive mood swings. With Bianca now missing and without her medication, concerns were heightened. Bianca, though only 13, had the physical presence of an older teenager, being five feet six inches tall and weighing 185 pounds. There were fears about how she might react without her medication, including potential confusion, hallucinations, or aggression.

Despite extensive police searches in the area where Bianca was last seen, they found no trace of her. Shannon strongly believed Bianca had been abducted, citing her daughter's naivety and potential to trust a stranger. This view, however, contrasted sharply with her earlier decision to let Bianca walk alone, prompting questions about her judgment and protective instincts.

In the close-knit community of their small town, Bianca's disappearance caused widespread concern and gossip. The family, desperate for answers, offered a reward, sparking a multitude of tips. Yet, each lead proved fruitless, leaving the mystery of Bianca's whereabouts unsolved.

Three months later, the situation took a disturbing turn. Shannon Tanner, already in the public eye due to her daughter's disappearance, was arrested under harrowing circumstances. She faced charges of a violent assault on her other daughter, who was 17. The allegations were severe, including being struck with a curling iron, physical beatings, and threats of confinement. When authorities arrived at the scene, they found Shannon physically restraining her daughter, requiring police intervention to halt the assault. This development cast a new, troubling light on the family dynamics and raised further questions about the circumstances surrounding Bianca's disappearance.

Shannon's arrest took a dramatic turn when she allegedly assaulted a deputy and tried to use a shard of glass as a weapon, leading to her being subdued by a taser. She was subsequently arrested and released on bond, but the incident severely tarnished her public reputation. The ensuing media coverage cast a suspicious light on her, fueling speculation about her involvement in her daughter Bianca's disappearance.

However, the police had already ruled Shannon out as a suspect in Bianca's case. Despite this, the recent alarming events significantly clouded public perception of her. The investigation into Bianca's disappearance hit a stalemate, with numerous leads and potential sightings all leading to dead ends. The police suspected local involvement, given the specific location of Bianca's last known whereabouts.

In 2007, there was a brief moment of hope when police investigated Michael Devlin, a man linked to the kidnapping of two other boys found in his house after years of captivity. Devlin was convicted for these crimes, and a task force explored possible connections to Bianca's case. Unfortunately, no ties were established, and the task force disbanded.

The tragedy was compounded by the death of Bianca's father in 2009, leaving her mother and sister grappling with the ongoing mystery. Various theories circulated, including a sighting of a white pickup truck near a pond the night Bianca vanished. In 2009, a startling claim by Tiffany, Bianca's sister and a victim of Shannon's assault, suggested Bianca might be in the pond, but this lead was fruitless.

In 2012, Tiffany was arrested for trafficking two high school girls, echoing the dark path she had been drawn into. Her silence about who introduced her to this underworld raised further questions about the family's complex dynamics.

This case remains mired in mystery and suspicion. Tiffany's cryptic remark about Bianca and the pond, the possibility of an escalated argument leading to tragedy, and the enigma of Tiffany's silence about her own abuser are all puzzling aspects of this case. The troubled family history, marked by abuse and secrets, underscores the often disturbing reality that in abduction cases, the perpetrator is frequently someone known to the victim. The convoluted nature of this case, with its unresolved questions and tragic turns, starkly illustrates this unsettling fact.

Lydia Abrams

In the sun-drenched valleys of Southern California, nestled near Mountain Center, Lydia Kenshallow emerged into the world on July 6, 1954. Affectionately known as Dia to those who knew her best, she spent her formative and adult years in the warm embrace of this region. Her life, a tapestry of love, luxury, and later, legal battles, began to unfold in vivid detail when she was 25. It was then that Dia's path intersected with Clem Abrams, a 39-year-old real estate mogul whose fortune was already counted in millions.

The pair's romance blossomed over five years, culminating in an engagement in 1984. Together, they welcomed two children into their lives, Clinton and Chris Sara. Clem, a titan in the realm of real estate, continued to amass wealth, significantly augmenting the family's opulent lifestyle. They owned and developed numerous properties sprawled across the 116-acre Bonita Vista Ranch in Idlewild, California, a dazzling jewel valued at several million dollars.

Dia, a nature enthusiast with a deep love for the outdoors, found her paradise on the ranch. She indulged in horse riding and hiking, embracing her love for animals by rescuing many. Those close to her described her as a spirited and caring soul, grounded in her connection to nature and passionate about animal welfare. Despite her down-to-earth persona, Dia never shied away from maintaining her appearance, a luxury easily afforded by her substantial wealth.

However, as the years rolled by, the once strong marriage began to unravel, leading to their separation. The complexities of their post-separation arrangement remained a mystery, but both Dia and Clem continued to reside on the Bonita Vista Ranch. Unbroken by the end of her marriage, Dia ventured back into the world of romance, eventually joining FarmersOnly.com. In 2016, she met Keith Harper, a man in his late 60s from Idaho with a background as colorful and troubled as the landscapes he hailed from.

Keith, a BYU graduate with multiple degrees, had a checkered past that included a rocky marital history, four children from a previous marriage, and a troubling criminal record involving sexual misconduct. Despite these red flags, Dia and Keith's relationship flourished rapidly, leading to Keith moving into the Bonita Vista Ranch within six months of their meeting.

However, tranquility was short-lived. In 2018, Clem's passing marked the beginning of a contentious legal battle within the Abrams family. Clem had designated his children as the executors and primary beneficiaries of his estate, leaving Dia with significantly less than she had grown accustomed to. Accustomed to a life of luxury and financial dependence on Clem for nearly four decades, this drastic change in circumstances was a bitter pill to swallow.

Dia, feeling wronged by the prenuptial agreement that she and Clem had signed in 1984, which effectively left her with little of Clem's wealth, decided to challenge it in court. She argued that the agreement was unfair, given that she had been discouraged from working and was not involved in managing their finances. The ranch, which she had tended to for years, was a particular point of contention, as she felt it rightfully belonged to her, not just Clem's children.

Dia contended that she had signed the prenup under duress. At that time, she was four months pregnant and just weeks away from their lavish, planned wedding. Guests had been invited, the venue booked and paid for, when Clem presented her with the prenup. Overwhelmed by the pressure of imminent motherhood and the societal expectations of a grand wedding, Dia felt cornered into signing the document.

Dia's lawyers later argued that the terms of the prenup were unconscionable. The agreement negated California's community property laws, which typically require the equal division of assets acquired during the marriage in the event of a divorce. Since Dia had been financially dependent on Clem throughout their marriage, not acquiring any substantial assets of her own, the prenup essentially left her with little to no claim on the wealth accumulated during their union.

Further complicating matters was the claim that the prenup violated public policy. Dia's legal team referenced laws dating back to 1872 to support this assertion. They argued that the agreement was fundamentally at odds with established legal principles, thereby invalidating it. In addition to challenging the prenup, Dia sought to modify Clem's trust. This aspect of the legal battle was even more intricate, involving a slew of arguments and legal maneuverings. Dia's goal was to secure a $6.7 million funding for the marital trust from Clem's estate, substantially more than what she was initially left with.

This legal battle stirred deep unrest within the Abrams family. Dia's children, Clinton and Chris Sara, stood in stark opposition to her claims. They filed a counter-petition, insisting that the original terms of the prenup and Clem's estate planning should be respected and upheld. This familial strife over the vast estate highlights the adage that money often complicates relationships, potentially leading to unhappiness and discord.

Amidst this tumultuous backdrop, a tragic twist occurred. On June 6, 2020, Dia vanished from the Bonita Vista Ranch, her whereabouts remaining a mystery to this day. That Saturday had started ordinarily, with Dia baking cinnamon rolls for a terminally ill neighbor. After delivering the baked goods, she returned home. Around 2 PM, she joined Keith for lunch at the main house on their property. Keith, who by then claimed to be engaged to Dia, recounted that their lunch was largely uneventful, save for Dia expressing a desire to discuss something important later.

After lunch, which concluded around 2:30 PM, Keith went to mow a meadow, expecting Dia to tend to their horses at a nearby property. When Dia didn't show up by 7:30 PM, Keith began to worry. Finding her phone and wallet in their bedroom, and her truck still at the residence, heightened his concerns. Keith contacted a highway patrolman, who advised that a formal missing person's report couldn't be filed until three days had passed. Deciding to wait, Keith spent a restless night hoping for Dia's return.

The next day, Dia still hadn't returned. Keith reached out to friends and neighbors, and soon a search party, including Dia's son Clinton, was organized. However, Keith's lack of participation in the search efforts raised suspicions. Isedro Garcia, a worker on the property, noted Keith's apathy and contrasted it with the kinder treatment he had received from Clem and Dia. Keith's reputation among the staff was poor; he was known for his harsh treatment and racial insensitivity.

On that fateful Sunday, Keith Harper's behavior was noticeably peculiar. His evasiveness and claims of unavoidable meetings raised suspicions among those searching for Dia Kenshallow. Despite his odd demeanor, the search for Dia continued relentlessly. Diana Feder, a close friend and neighbor of Dia's, assumed a pivotal role in coordinating the search efforts. Diana's involvement would later prove to be a complex layer in this unfolding mystery.

The vastness of the Kenshallow property posed a significant challenge for the search teams. With acres of land to comb through, they scoured every inch for any sign of Dia or clues to her disappearance. However, their efforts were in vain, and Dia was officially reported missing to the Riverside Sheriff's Department.

The following day, as the official police investigation commenced, Keith's actions became even more bewildering. In a move that stunned everyone, he abruptly left California in his RV, heading to Arizona. Keith claimed he had to address a tax issue related to a property he owned there. The timing of his departure, coinciding with the intensification of the search for Dia, only deepened the aura of suspicion surrounding him.

The investigative team, undeterred by Keith's absence, embarked on a thorough search of the 116-acre ranch. Various teams, including missing persons and homicide units, alongside divers, were mobilized. Several search warrants were executed, covering the primary residence, a secondary property on the ranch, Keith's storage facility in New Mexico, and his RV.

The search revealed intriguing findings. In the main house, items such as a bed sheet with possible blood stains, spent bullet casings, handwritten letters, and a Netgear router were discovered. A subsequent warrant led to the discovery of a sizable illegal marijuana operation on the property, consisting of over 2,300 plants and 357 pounds of processed marijuana. Keith denied any knowledge of this operation, which, according to the police, bore no connection to Dia's disappearance.

Meanwhile, the search expanded to Keith's business interests in Arizona and New Mexico. While specifics of what was found during these searches remain undisclosed, it was noted that the RV was seized and examined thoroughly, with the front seat being removed for evidence.

As the investigation deepened, the dynamics within the Kenshallow family grew increasingly complex. Dia's children, Clinton and Chris Sara, were initially given control of the property. However, this decision soon became contentious due to Dia's recent amendments to her trust and power of attorney. Just 15 days before her disappearance, Dia had made significant changes to these documents. She removed her children entirely, appointing Keith as the primary trustee and Diana Feder as an alternate. The revisions also named Keith as a beneficiary in the event of her death.

The abrupt nature of these changes, occurring in the midst of a heated legal battle over Clem's will, cast a shadow of doubt over the motivations and circumstances surrounding the amendments. The children, suspecting foul play, contested the validity of these documents in court.

As part of their legal challenge, Clinton and Chris Sara highlighted several irregularities. The power of attorney document appeared incomplete, lacked Dia's signature, and had inconsistencies in its formatting. They argued that these anomalies indicated the document was fraudulent, further questioning Keith and Diana's fitness to assume control of Dia's estate.

The unfolding drama took another turn when Keith hired an organization named Find Me, which used psychics in their investigation. While psychics are often a controversial and unreliable source in criminal investigations, Keith asserted that they had identified the killer and the location of Dia's body. However, his inability to recall critical details from their report cast further doubt on his credibility.

In a strange twist, Keith eventually claimed to remember that Dia was allegedly murdered by a man named Patrick Griffin, hired by her son Clinton. This accusation, combined with the lack of concrete evidence and the already cleared Hemet Lake as the supposed location of Dia's body, only added to the surreal and convoluted nature of the case.

Throughout this ordeal, Diana Feder's actions were also under scrutiny. As a key figure in managing Dia's Airbnb properties and her sudden armed vigilance at the main house, suspicions arose about her potential involvement and motives.

Yet, amidst the whirlpool of accusations, a different theory has emerged, suggesting that Dia's son, Clinton, might have played a role in her mysterious vanishing. This alternate narrative, primarily propagated by Keith, points to a potential motive rooted in familial discord and financial disputes.

According to Keith, in the months leading up to Dia's disappearance, she expressed grave concerns about her safety, specifically fearing her son Clinton. These fears, as Keith alleges, were linked to Dia's attempts to alter Clem's will, which she believed might provoke a violent reaction from Clinton. This looming sense of danger was reportedly shared with Keith and a circle of Dia's friends. It's important to note that these claims have not been substantiated beyond Keith's statements and lack concrete evidence.

Keith further claims that Dia planned to discuss these fears with him on the day of her disappearance, suggesting that her concerns about Clinton were pressing and deeply troubling. This narrative, however, is complicated by the lack of direct communication from Dia confirming these fears, leaving much of Keith's story open to skepticism.

Adding another layer to this complex saga, Keith asserts that Clinton once attempted to harm Dia in the past, alleging an incident involving poisoning that supposedly left Dia in a coma. This serious accusation, however, lacks corroboration from Dia herself or any police reports, making it difficult to assess its credibility.

Amidst these accusations, Clinton's relationship with his mother comes under scrutiny. Despite claims from Isedro, a worker on the property, that Clinton rarely visited the ranch, Clinton maintains that he and his mother shared a close and loving bond, regularly communicating and expressing affection. This contradiction between Clinton's account and the observations of others further muddies the waters in understanding the true nature of their relationship.

Complicating matters, Clinton alleges the discovery of a bloody pillow in a truck formerly owned by Clem, which he claims to have found shortly after

Dia's disappearance. This claim, though publicly stated by Clinton, lacks independent verification or confirmation from law enforcement, casting doubt on its veracity.

The battle of narratives between Keith and Clinton is a tangled web of accusations and counter-accusations. Both men present theories that implicate the other, each bolstered by a mix of conjecture, hearsay, and scant evidence. Keith's departure from the state during the investigation, his alleged involvement with Dia's trust and power of attorney changes, and his curious behavior all paint him as a suspect in the eyes of many. On the other hand, Clinton's strained relationship with Dia, as portrayed by Keith, and the unverified claim of a bloody pillow found in the truck, raise questions about his potential involvement.

In the midst of this bewildering case, the truth about Dia Kenshallow's fate remains shrouded in mystery. The ongoing investigation, marred by conflicting stories and a lack of definitive evidence, continues to baffle those seeking answers. As each twist and turn in the narrative unfolds, the search for clarity and closure in this perplexing case goes on, leaving more questions than answers in its wake.

Matthew Weaver Jr

Matthew Weaver Jr.'s story unfolds like a tapestry of complexity and mystery, woven against the vibrant backdrop of Simi Valley, California, part of the bustling Greater Los Angeles area. Born on April 2, 1997, Matthew's early years were marked by a significant family change; his parents parted ways, leaving him to be nurtured by the guiding hand of his father, Matthew Weaver Sr. In these formative years, his father's remarriage introduced Brooke into young Matthew's life, a new maternal figure.

As the chapters of Matthew's life turned, he encountered the often turbulent waters of personal relationships. In a bold move, he relocated to New York, following the beats of his heart to live with a romantic partner. Yet, fate had other plans; the relationship crumbled, leaving Matthew grappling with the elusive specter of stability. Eventually, he retraced his steps back to California, finding solace and a place to call home in his grandmother's abode.

A heart brimming with compassion, Matthew's affinity for animals led him to rescue and nurture a dog, a furry companion in his journey of life. But as 2018 dawned, a year when he would turn 21, his life seemed to be fraying at the edges. The end of a romantic relationship heralded a descent into a more chaotic existence. Matthew's days became a whirlwind of drug and alcohol use, missed work commitments, and relentless partying.

In a bid for independence, April of that year saw Matthew moving into his own space in Granada Hills, approximately 18 miles from the familiarity of Simi Valley. His professional life also took a turn, as he began working on power lines, following in the occupational footsteps of his father.

The mystery deepens as we delve into the timeline of Matthew's disappearance. On the evening of August 9, 2018, he visited his workplace to collect a part of his wages in cash. Following this, he stopped by his father's home, where an ominous moment unfolded; Matthew requested to see his father's pistol, snapping a photo of it for Snapchat with a chilling caption: "Game over."

He then spoke of a new romantic interest, Melissa, and left to meet her. Their night was a blur of stops at Walmart, a gas station, and alleged purchases of cocaine and marijuana. They meandered through the night, partying, before Matthew parked outside Melissa's home. In a raw display of emotion, he confided in her, tears revealing the unhappiness and turmoil within. Melissa, somewhat taken aback by the intensity of the encounter, didn't perceive their connection as Matthew did.

In the early hours of August 10, Matthew departed from Melissa's place. However, instead of heading east towards his apartment, he veered south, towards the Santa Monica Mountains. Driving off the 101 freeway in Calabasas and onto the winding paths of Mulholland Highway, he entered a more secluded, rural landscape. Stunt Road beckoned him, leading to the intersection with Saddle Peak Road at Topanga Canyon, known for its breathtaking scenic lookout.

Near this spot lay an access road, usually barred by a locked metal gate. But fate, it seems, left the gate unlocked. Matthew's BMW was last seen on surveillance footage, passing through the gate around 7:15 am, the lone vehicle in the desolate expanse of that early morning.

This road, a transformation from asphalt to a challenging dirt trail, lay nestled in the Santa Monica Mountains, an area familiar yet unpredictable. The road, notorious for its sharp turns adjacent to steep drop-offs, eventually narrowed to a point where driving further became an impossibility. Despite his familiarity with the area's scenic overlooks, Matthew found himself in a daunting predicament.

Trapped by the mountain's rugged embrace, Matthew's car was ensnared by an unyielding small boulder, with one tire perilously dangling over the mountain's edge. In this isolated spot, where the road refused passage, he found himself unable to turn his vehicle around, the path behind as impenetrable as the one ahead.

At 8:10 a.m., in a bid for connection, Matthew reached out to his father, but the call went unanswered, echoing into the void. By 11:48 a.m., he contacted Melissa, but she was at work and could only respond via text. Matthew's message to her was cryptic and laced with urgency: "Like some crazy going on, blank going on." At 11:50 a.m., he sent another message, incomplete and frantic, "I just to talk while I have the chance," as if the words were a hurried thought, a plea for understanding.

Following these messages, Matthew's communication ceased, his phone either turned off or succumbed to a drained battery. Melissa's replies at 12:54 p.m. and again at 4:25 p.m., inquiring about his well-being, floated unanswered into the digital ether.

The mystery deepened the following day, August 11, at 1:11 a.m., when hikers in the vicinity reported hearing calls for help from both a male and a female. This prompted an immediate police response. The search, however, revealed no one in distress. Instead, what they discovered was Matthew's abandoned BMW, a silent witness to his unexplained absence. Despite extensive searches by police and volunteers, Matthew remained an enigma, his whereabouts a baffling uncertainty.

Months later, a glimmer of hope or perhaps a deeper mystery surfaced. A baseball cap, resembling the one Matthew wore, was discovered in the area, alongside a torn t-shirt, possibly his. A blood test on the t-shirt yielded inconclusive results, deepening the enigma. The puzzle gained another piece on January 27, 2019, when a hiker found the key to Matthew's BMW, lying 75 feet from where his car had been immobilized.

On the night of September 7, 2020, around 8:21 pm, the quiet town of Sylmar was jolted from its usual tranquility by an alarming incident. The police, responding to a report of a stolen car, were unexpectedly met with gunfire as they arrived at the scene. Matthew Weaver Sr., father of the missing Matthew Weaver Jr., was the man behind the trigger. In a shocking turn of events, the officers were forced to abandon their cruisers and seek cover, miraculously avoiding any injuries.

In a bewildering sequence of actions, Matthew Sr. seized this moment of chaos to commandeer one of the police vehicles. With a perplexing calmness, he toyed with the vehicle's lights, an act that seemed to convey a message beyond mere defiance. His actions then took an even more erratic turn as he aimlessly wandered into a nearby drainage ditch. The clock struck 12:03 am on September 8, marking the moment when a substantial contingent of law enforcement officers succeeded in apprehending Matthew Weaver Sr.

This incident led to speculation among observers and those close to the family. Some theorized that Matthew Sr.'s erratic behavior could have stemmed from a mental health crisis, possibly triggered by the unrelenting stress and agony caused by his son's baffling disappearance. There was a palpable sense of frustration directed towards the police, perceived by Matthew Sr. as indifferent or insufficient in their efforts to find his missing son. Ironically, the massive police response to his own arrest might have been, in his perspective, a twisted vindication of his attempt to capture their attention.

Shifting the lens to Matthew Weaver Jr.'s disappearance, various theories have surfaced in an attempt to unravel the mystery. One such theory suggests that Matthew might have intentionally disappeared to start anew. This hypothesis, however, seems implausible given his disorganized state and lack of preparation for such a drastic step. Matthew was struggling to manage his everyday life, making the idea of him orchestrating a new identity and life far-fetched. Moreover, he left behind essential items, including his motor vehicle, which would have been crucial for a fresh start.

Another prevailing theory considers the possibility of foul play, with Matthew potentially falling victim to criminals, perhaps linked to his involvement with drugs. This theory is somewhat bolstered by Matthew's apparent desire to arm himself, as evidenced by his interest in his father's pistol and his attempts to acquire a firearm from a friend. The cryptic message about "some crazy going on" and the reports of screams in the mountains add layers of complexity to this hypothesis. However, the absence of other vehicles in the surveillance footage of the area where Matthew's BMW was found casts doubt on this scenario.

The third, and perhaps the most compelling theory, is that Matthew succumbed to a tragic fate in the mountains, either by his own hand or due to natural elements. His desperation for a firearm and his emotional state, coupled with the ominous "game over" social media post, could suggest a plan to end his life. His substance use and the possibility of him being in a psychotic state, potentially exacerbated by a recent head injury, further support this theory.

In weighing these theories, the likelihood seems to tilt towards Matthew meeting a solitary end in the mountains, with self-harm or exposure being the most probable causes. The notion of murder, although possible, appears less likely, and the idea of Matthew starting a new life seems the least probable.

Reflecting on Matthew's story, one can't help but ponder the devastating impact of substance abuse. While Matthew acknowledged his struggle with addiction, it's possible that those around him might have been in denial about the severity of his situation. Substance abuse, often a coping mechanism for underlying emotional turmoil, can provide temporary relief but ultimately leads to deeper, more destructive problems. Matthew's story is a somber reminder of the profound consequences of unaddressed emotional pain and substance dependency.

Christopher Kerze

Christopher Kerze, born on February 19, 1973, would have celebrated his 48th birthday this year. His mysterious case unfolds on April 20, 1990, in the quiet town of Eagan, Minnesota. At just 17 years old, Christopher lived with his parents in their cozy family home. Known for his academic excellence, Christopher was not only a stellar student but had also earned recognition as a National Honor Society invitee and a National Scholar Semi-Finalist. His interests were as diverse as they were engaging, spanning from an avid love for reading to a keen fascination with computers, and an enthusiastic indulgence in outdoor activities like skiing and camping.

On the fateful day of April 20, 1990, the Kerze household was slightly unusual. Christopher's father, Jim, was away on a business trip, leaving Christopher and his mother, Joanie, alone at home. That morning, Christopher complained of a severe headache and decided to stay home from school. His mother, caring and concerned, gave him some painkillers and left him to rest at home, expecting him to recover by the afternoon.

Upon their return later that day, a sense of unease crept over Christopher's parents. The family's light blue 1988 Dodge Caravan was nowhere in the driveway. Inside the house, the family dog paced alone, and a cryptic note lay on the kitchen table. Penned by Christopher, it read: "Mum, something important came up & feeling somewhat better. Back by six (unless I get lost)." The word "lost" was ominously underlined twice. The family assumed he had gone for a drive, a common pastime during which he occasionally lost his way.

However, Christopher never returned, and no one heard from him again. On the day he vanished, he was dressed distinctively in a mid-calf length, acid-washed, light blue denim trench coat, a large black sweatshirt, and either blue or black Bugle Boy jeans with unique knee pockets. He wore size 29M, a black leather belt, and white socks, complemented by either size 11 or 11.5 brown leather boat shoes. Notably, he sported a plastic zebra-print Swatch watch and likely carried a driver's license in a black bi-fold leather wallet.

On the day he vanished, it was revealed that Christopher had covertly withdrawn $200 from his savings account, unbeknownst to his parents. This act alone raised many questions about his intentions. Adding to the enigma, his parents realized that his father's Mossberg 20-gauge bolt-action shotgun was missing from their home. Strangely, though the shotgun was gone, there was no sign that any ammunition had been taken along with it.

The day after Christopher's disappearance brought another bewildering twist. A letter arrived at the Kerze family home, postmarked from Duluth, a town in Minnesota approximately two and a half hours' drive from the Kerze residence in Eagan. This letter, penned by Christopher himself, contained startling confessions and apologies. He admitted to fabricating the story about his headache, a ruse to ensure he was left alone at home, granting him access to the family's Dodge Caravan. His words were cryptic: he had wanted to "get away to not even I know where." The letter, while expressing remorse to his family, frustratingly offered no clue as to his whereabouts or intended destination.

Two days into the investigation, a significant clue emerged. The Kerze family's Dodge Caravan was found abandoned in Northern Minnesota, on a lonely stretch of road in Itasca County, near the expansive wilderness of the George Washington State Forest and Chippewa National Forest. This discovery led authorities to theorize that Christopher had embarked on a 200-mile journey, concluding near Grand Rapids, Minnesota, before mysteriously abandoning the vehicle on the outskirts of the area. Notably, Christopher's grandparents resided in Grand Rapids at the time, adding another layer of intrigue to his chosen destination.

The convergence of these findings – the withdrawn money, the missing shotgun, the heartfelt letter, and the abandoned family vehicle – painted a complex and confusing picture. Christopher's actions and decisions in the days leading up to his disappearance were fraught with contradictions and unanswered questions, leaving both his family and the authorities grappling with the unknown.

In an intensive search, authorities scoured the vehicle and found yet another note. Unlike the previous letter sent to his parents, this note was brief and primarily served to identify the vehicle's ownership for anyone who might find it. Despite this clue, there was no clear indication of what had happened to Christopher after he left the car.

Given the rugged terrain surrounding the area where the car was found, it was plausible that Christopher could have embarked on foot in any direction. This possibility presented a daunting challenge for the authorities, as pinpointing his exact route seemed almost impossible. Compounding the mystery, there was no trace of his father's shotgun. The prevailing theory suggested Christopher might have discarded the weapon in one of the nearby forests. Hoping to find some direction, investigators appealed to locals, particularly hunters and hikers, for any information about a found gun.

In the immediate aftermath of Christopher's disappearance, his family and law enforcement officials launched a widespread campaign to find him. Posters bearing his image were distributed extensively, urging the public to keep an eye out. Despite Christopher's seemingly stable and successful academic life, his reasons for leaving remained elusive. Some speculated about potential mental health issues, including suicidal ideation, but these theories were never substantiated and met with skepticism by those who knew him well.

The case took a strange turn in 2004, almost 14 years after Christopher's disappearance. The Eagan Police Department received an anonymous letter urging them to cease their search, assuring that Christopher would return on his own terms when ready. The authenticity and origin of this letter, whether it was from Christopher or an uninvolved third party, remained unverified.

Around the same time, Christopher's parents and his close friend and neighbor reported receiving numerous silent phone calls. These calls, often characterized by background noise resembling a party, would abruptly end whenever they attempted to speak. These occurrences fueled speculation and hope among Christopher's family that he might be trying to reach out.

Despite the scarcity of leads and the challenging nature of the investigation, Christopher's family never ceased in their quest for answers. In 2016, a significant development in an unrelated case reignited interest in long-unsolved disappearances. The resolution of the Jacob Wetterling case, a boy who vanished in 1989 near Minneapolis and whose abductor confessed in 2016, brought renewed attention to Christopher's case. Though not directly linked, the solving of Jacob Wetterling's case inspired hope that perhaps, like Jacob's, the cold case of Christopher Kerze might one day find closure.

Eugene Martin

Eugene Martin, affectionately known as Gene by his family and friends, first saw the light of day on August 17, 1970. As a child, he was the epitome of politeness, tinged with a quiet, shy demeanor. Despite his reserved nature, Gene was a beacon of energy, immersing himself in a plethora of activities. He had a particular fondness for football, skateboarding, and fishing – pursuits that echoed the typical joys of childhood.

As the 1980s dawned, Gene, like many of his peers, was captivated by the emerging world of video games. When not enthralled by digital adventures, he was often found engrossed in the latest television shows, ranging from sports broadcasts to the animated wonders of Saturday morning cartoons. His mother, Janice, fondly reminisced about his hobbies, noting his unyielding enthusiasm for skateboarding despite frequent scrapes and bruises. She marveled at his resilience, always ready to hop back on his board after a fall.

Outside of leisure, Gene was not one to shy away from responsibility. In the pursuit of earning some extra pocket money, he embarked on an early morning job. Together with his older brother Don, Gene would rise at dawn to collect and distribute newspapers. His choice of employment was with the Des Moines Register, a gig he had only recently taken up in May.

Gene's familial life was complex yet filled with affection. He was born to Donald and Janice Martin, but at the time of a pivotal event in his life, he was residing with his father, Donald. After a move in April, and Donald's subsequent remarriage, Gene's family expanded to include five half-brothers and two half-sisters. Despite the potential challenges of a blended family, the love for the thirteen-year-old was unanimous. His siblings fondly regarded him as the 'baby' of the family, a beloved figure they felt compelled to protect and cherish.

As August 12th loomed, a sense of excitement permeated the Martin household. The Iowa State Fair was in town, and Gene eagerly anticipated using his hard-earned money for rides and games. Furthermore, his 14th birthday was just around the corner, unbeknownst to him, his father had planned to surprise him with a brand new bike. The family was buzzing with anticipation for the celebration.

However, destiny had other plans. Just five days before his birthday, Gene mysteriously vanished in the early hours while on his newspaper delivery route. On the night of August 11th, Gene had enjoyed a movie with friends, returning home early to rest up for his morning job. His brother Don, typically his companion on the route, was away at a friend's house, leaving Gene to undertake the task alone.

The morning of August 12th began like any other for Gene. He woke up on time, preparing for work without disturbing anyone in the house. His father, Donald, later recalled hearing the alarm but not Gene getting ready. After getting dressed, Gene set off to the corner of Southwest 14th Street and High View Drive, the starting point for his deliveries.

Connie Clowenberch, an early riser heading out for golf, noticed Gene sitting at the corner with his empty paper bag. Around 5:10 AM, Connie waved to Gene, who waved back, with nothing seeming amiss. Gene then began his routine of preparing the newspapers for delivery, folding and banding them before loading his carrier bag.

Paul Porter, the route manager, later reported seeing Gene's bag full of papers but not Gene himself. He assumed Gene was making deliveries nearby. However, when customers began to call, complaining about undelivered newspapers, Porter realized something was amiss. Returning to the scene, he found Gene's bag untouched.

At approximately 7:15 AM, with no sign of Gene, Porter called Donald Martin to report the situation. After a fruitless search of the house and the city, Donald, joined by his brother Ron, scoured the area on motorcycles, searching malls, schools, and other likely spots. Unfortunately, their efforts were in vain.

Upon returning home, a distraught Donald contacted the police, triggering an immediate and extensive search. This case bore eerie similarities to the disappearance of Johnny Gosch just two years earlier, prompting a rapid response from authorities. The Des Moines police deployed tactical unit officers and detectives, aided by local volunteers, including the Capital City Knights football team, to search for Gene. A "fact sheet" bearing Gene's details and image was distributed to aid the search efforts.

The rapid dissemination of Gene's information across various departments highlighted the urgency of the situation. Sergeant Mullins of the Des Moines police department coordinated a city-wide effort to circulate details about the missing boy to all patrol cars, ensuring that every officer on the street was aware and on the lookout.

The initial search commenced at around 8:40 AM, a mere three hours after the last confirmed sighting of Gene. News of his disappearance swiftly rippled through the city, amplifying the urgency of the search. Focus was primarily centered in the southwest area, where Gene's abandoned newspaper bag was discovered. This led investigators to believe that Gene might still be in the vicinity, or at least they clung to that hope.

At first, authorities grappled with the nature of Gene's disappearance. Was it a simple case of a lost child or something more sinister? The possibility of Gene getting distracted and wandering off was considered, but as the search intensified, this theory seemed less plausible.

In a bid to enhance the safety of their carriers, the Des Moines Register, where Gene was employed, had previously implemented a carrier safety training program. This initiative was in response to the disappearance of Johnny Gosch, another paper carrier, two years earlier. The Register responded to Gene's disappearance with a substantial reward offer, initially setting it at $5,000 and later increasing it to $25,000 for any information leading to his location. They also took additional measures, like placing notices in the newspapers and instructing carriers to be vigilant of any suspicious activities on their routes. Supervisors were deployed to oversee the carriers as they performed their duties.

While a theory of Gene running away due to a domestic dispute briefly surfaced, it was quickly dismissed by the police. Within hours, the investigation leaned towards a more alarming possibility: abduction. Officers canvassed Gene's delivery route, going door-to-door, seeking any information from residents about unusual sightings or encounters.

Among the emerging leads was a report about a decrepit green car, seen in the vicinity of 14th and 18th streets on the morning of Gene's disappearance. The car, reportedly driven by a scruffy-looking man in his late twenties or early thirties, was last seen around the time Gene would have started his paper route. Another witness reported seeing a man engaged in what seemed like a friendly conversation with Gene. This mysterious individual was described in vague terms, posing a challenge for investigators.

The police's determination to avoid a repeat of the initial missteps in Johnny Gosch's case led them to swiftly engage federal authorities. Special Agent Herbert Hawkins of the FBI's Omaha office arrived in Des Moines with a team of 16 agents to assist in the search and investigation. The media played a crucial role in disseminating information, with local newspapers, radio, and TV channels actively covering Gene's disappearance. This media attention led to a flood of calls to the police, each one meticulously followed up.

The search for Gene expanded beyond his delivery route to isolated areas across the city, including parks, warehouses, and riverfronts. Despite the expanded search team, which now included 25 Des Moines police officers, 16 FBI agents, and numerous local volunteers, leads were frustratingly scarce. However, the resolve to find Gene remained unwavering.

As the search continued, mass-produced flyers featuring Gene's photo and details circulated widely. The importance of the initial hours after a disappearance was underscored by Sergeant Mullins, emphasizing the decreasing likelihood of solving a case as time passes.

The Gosch family, still reeling from their own tragedy, reached out to the Martins, offering support and urging them to keep Gene's story in the public eye. They emphasized the grim reality that the perpetrator of their son's abduction was still at large, possibly indicating a sinister pattern in Des Moines' history.

On the following Monday, August 13th, the Des Moines Police Department took a decisive step to streamline their efforts in finding Gene Martin by es-tablishing a dedicated hotline for tips related to his disappearance. The phone lines buzzed continuously, with hundreds of calls flooding in. A significant number of these calls were from concerned citizens offering suggestions on potential search locations rather than providing direct information about the abduction.

That very day, a man made his way to the Martin family home with a possibly crucial observation. He recounted seeing a young boy, who bore marks of bruising, in a car near 14th Street. Having seen Gene's flyer, he felt compelled to report this sighting, thinking it might be connected to Gene's case. However, this lead, like many others, failed to develop into anything substantial.

The following day, Tuesday, August 14th, the police interviewed a person who had been spotted in the area on the morning of Gene's disappearance. This individual, the driver of the green car that had been sighted, was brought in for questioning. Despite high hopes, the police's investigation hit a wall; they could not establish any link between this man and Gene's abduction. In an in-depth investigation, the police verified his alibi - he had been dropping off his wife at work - and subsequently cleared him from the list of suspects.

During this period, rumors circulated about the discovery of blood near where Gene was last seen, intensifying the atmosphere of apprehension. However, these reports were soon dismissed as unfounded rumors. The police took this opportunity to stress the importance of accuracy and caution in the information being shared with them, highlighting the dangers of speculation and sensationalism in such sensitive cases.

Meanwhile, the community rallied together in a remarkable show of solidarity. Volunteers from all corners of the city joined organized search parties. Two young boys from Gene's neighborhood devoted their Monday afternoon to distributing flyers. Gene's uncle, Roger Blanchard, took the initiative to organize more extensive search parties that ventured further into the city and its surroundings, exploring wooded and grassland areas, including places like Walnut Wood State Park.

Late in the evening, the police received an anonymous tip from a caller who claimed to have seen Gene conversing with the unidentified man, the one allegedly associated with the 1972 or 73 green Chevrolet Malibu. The caller described a chilling detail - the man had placed his hands on Gene at least once during their interaction. However, choosing to remain anonymous, the caller's motivation was solely to assist the case.

By Wednesday, August 15th, the FBI focused on tracking down this same man, believed to be a key figure in the case. A specialist was flown in from Washington to conduct re-interviews with the six witnesses, in hopes of compiling a detailed artist's composite of the man. While he was not labeled a suspect, his connection to the case was of high interest to the authorities.

On the same day, Gene's parents had a meeting scheduled with Governor Terry Branstad, who took a personal interest in the case. At this juncture, the search for Gene expanded beyond city limits, with additional resources being requested from surrounding police departments. One of the searches included members of the Civil Air Patrol, combing through the dense wilderness southwest of the city, a line of searchers stretched out over 200 yards wide.

In a significant development, the police recovered a tennis shoe and a pair of shorts near where Gene was last seen. Initially, this discovery sparked hope of a breakthrough, but it was soon determined that neither item belonged to Gene, resetting the investigation back to square one.

The reward for information leading to Gene increased to $30,000, thanks to contributions from the Iowa Newspaper Association. Following their meeting with Governor Branstad, Donald Martin expressed gratitude for the governor's concern and involvement. The Martin family was granted unprecedented access to the investigation, a gesture from Tom Ruxlow, the chief of the Iowa Division of Criminal Investigations.

Reporters sought Donald Martin's insight into who might have taken his son. Donald reflected on Gene's character, highlighting his shyness and reluctance to interact with strangers. This insight shaped the narrative of the investigation, suggesting that the abductor was someone Gene might have trusted.

Special Agent Hawkins, however, expressed frustration at the lack of evidence to construct a comprehensive psychological profile of the abductor. The absence of a crime scene and physical evidence hindered their ability to deeply understand the perpetrator's psyche.

As the investigation progressed, the frustration among law enforcement was palpable. Sergeant Mullins voiced this sentiment, acknowledging the lack of concrete evidence or witnesses. This type of investigation, he noted, could be protracted, requiring painstaking efforts to follow each lead.

By Thursday, August 16th, the search had become increasingly desperate. Volunteers and police scoured the city and its outskirts, searching through garbage cans and dumpsters, hoping to find any clue linked to Gene. Police accompanied garbage trucks, examining over 4,800 homes' trash, yet their efforts yielded no significant leads.

Around the same time, a large search operation was launched in the Ankeny industrial district, south of Orlabor Road. The operation included a search helicopter and a substantial contingent of federal, state, and local law enforcement.

In the wake of Gene Martin's disappearance, the Des Moines Police Department swiftly set up a dedicated hotline to gather tips. This move resulted in an outpouring of calls, mostly from community members eager to suggest potential search areas, though tangible leads about the crime were scarce.

The search efforts intensified significantly following a call to the hotline, prompting a late-night search in a cornfield about 15 miles north of Gene's last known location. The search was exhaustive, stretching into the early hours and resuming later in the morning, only to conclude on the subsequent Friday afternoon.

In an unexpected turn of events, President Ronald Reagan personally reached out to the Des Moines Register, offering his support and expressing sympathy. He agreed to help distribute Gene's missing person flyer nationwide, particularly in post offices. Eventually, the National Center for Missing and Exploited Children collaborated with the police to distribute the flyers through their network.

Simultaneously, the local police partnered with newspapers in the area to develop a program aimed at ensuring the safety of paper carriers. This initiative focused on educating carriers and their families about the potential risks of abduction, reinforcing safety protocols.

August 17th, which should have been a day of celebration for Gene's 14th birthday, was instead marked by a somber hope for his safe return. His parents, amidst their anguish, decided to preserve his birthday cake in the freezer, intending to save it for his homecoming.

Six days after Gene's disappearance, the police continued their diligent search. The authorities affirmed their commitment to the case, with officers' days off canceled to provide additional support for the search. Despite the influx of tips, many of which came from self-proclaimed psychics, the police struggled to track down each lead, finding this aspect of the investigation particularly taxing.

A local grocery chain made an effort to raise awareness by producing shopping bags featuring the images of both Gene and Johnny Gosch, another missing child. As time progressed, the number of volunteers dwindled, posing a challenge to sustain large-scale search efforts.

Sergeant Mullins of the Des Moines Police Department emphasized the ongoing need for volunteers, especially for searches in remote areas. He expressed a belief that there were people with valuable information who had yet to come forward.

Towards the end of August, volunteer numbers significantly decreased. A group consisting mainly of family, friends, and local students showed up to assist in a search along the Raccoon River. Despite these efforts, the investigation was losing momentum, with the case gradually going cold.

Local churches got involved, encouraging their congregations to participate in search efforts. The reward for information leading to Gene continued to rise, hitting $88,500, yet no breakthrough information was forthcoming.

Eventually, the police announced they were no longer seeking volunteers, having thoroughly searched all the major areas with their help. However, Sergeant Mullins assured that the investigation was still active, even though they were not actively seeking volunteer assistance.

Donald Martin, Gene's father, remained resolute in his hope for his son's return. In early September, the reward reached $111,000, raising hopes that this substantial amount might entice someone with crucial information to step forward.

However, as months passed, the investigation into Gene's disappearance began to grow cold. In October, a probe was initiated into the staff of the Des Moines Register following allegations of sexual assaults involving some of the younger carriers. Despite a late December article about the probe, no significant developments arose.

Financial strains began to take a toll on the Martin family by February of 1985. They had invested heavily in various efforts to find Gene, including hiring private investigators and consulting psychics. Des Moines Police Chief William Mulder commented on the limited usefulness of tips from psychics, noting their vagueness and lack of actionable details.

Time continued to pass with no new leads or developments, leaving the Martin family in a state of constant vigilance and uncertainty. They conducted yard sales and accepted donations, trying to maintain their search efforts, but the financial burden continued to grow.

In March 1986, another boy, Mark James Warren Allen, disappeared in similar circumstances, but, like Gene, he was never found. This, along with several attempted abductions in Des Moines, raised concerns about multiple predators operating in the area, though no direct links to Gene, Johnny, or Mark were ever established.

For many years, a ritual formed between Donald Martin and Detective Jim Rowley. Every Friday evening, they would meet to delve into the ongoing investigation of Gene Martin's disappearance. In these meetings, Donald would often bring forward questions, suggestions, and insights, all of which Rowley diligently pursued, no matter how slender the lead.

Rowley, in a candid conversation with Local 5 Iowa News, shared the depth of his commitment to the case. He recalled that regardless of the nature of the lead – whether it seemed promising or far-fetched – he would exhaustively follow it up. However, despite his relentless efforts, he admitted that none of the leads they chased bore any concrete evidence or reliability. They often turned out to be cases of mistaken identity or unproductive wild goose chases.

During his tenure on the case, Rowley ventured far beyond the local area, traveling to both Canada and Mexico in pursuit of leads. He estimated that over the course of his career, he had followed up on between two and three thousand leads, but none led to a credible or solid clue.

Rowley held his own theories about the case. He believed there was a connection between the abductions of Johnny Gosch and Gene Martin, possibly pointing to the same individual or a group being involved in both cases. Despite the lack of tangible evidence to prove his theory, he also speculated that both boys might have been tragically killed shortly after their abductions. This case, Rowley mentioned, was one that he would carry with him for the rest of his life. It was different from other cases, such as homicides or robberies, because it involved a young boy who vanished while simply delivering newspapers.

On December 27, 2010, Donald Martin passed away after a long struggle with Alzheimer's disease and colon cancer. To those who knew him, it was clear that finding Gene had become the central focus of his life. His quest to uncover the truth led him to become increasingly withdrawn over the years. He spent less time with friends and eventually divorced his wife Sue, dedicating all his spare time to the search for his son. Donald was only 65 years old at the time of his passing.

Gene's mother, Janice, had passed away a few years earlier due to complications related to diabetes. Both parents departed this world without ever learning the fate of their youngest child.

In September of 2016, Gene's brother, Mike, spoke with KCCI Des Moines News about his brother's case. Mike expressed the profound impact that not knowing what happened to Gene had on his life. He described a persistent feeling of emptiness and longing for closure. Mike remarked on the hardship of living with the unknown, a reality that had cast a shadow over his heart. He yearned for a moment of clarity, to finally understand what happened to his brother.

Mike also mentioned that it had been 12 years since the family had received any new information about Gene's disappearance. At the time of his disappearance, Eugene Wade Martin was described as a white male with brown hair and eyes, standing five feet tall and weighing around 110 pounds. He had a scar on his right knee and a previously fractured wrist. Gene was last seen wearing blue Genes, a gray and white striped midriff t-shirt with red sleeves, and blue Tracks brand shoes. Fortunately, DNA was available for analysis in the case, which could prove crucial if new evidence surfaced.

Witness sightings last placed Gene near Southwest 14th Street and High View Drive in Des Moines, where he was seen speaking to an unidentified older man. This lingering mystery, despite the passage of time and the efforts of family and law enforcement, remains an open wound, a haunting question mark in the lives of those who knew and loved Gene Martin.

Jayme Closs

In the small, close-knit community of Barron, Wisconsin, the Closs family was well-known and respected. Jayme Lynn Closs, born in 2005, was the cherished only child of James and Denise Closs. Her world was shattered in a horrific series of events that began in October 2018.

Jake Patterson, a man with a sinister plan, targeted the Closs family home with the intent to kidnap young Jayme. His first attempt to execute this plan was thwarted by activity within the house, leading him to fear being identified by potential witnesses. Undeterred, Patterson returned two days later, only to abort his mission once again for the same reason. The nightmare reached its climax on October 15, when Patterson, determined and now armed with a shotgun, made his third and final approach.

Under the cover of night, at approximately 12:53 a.m. Central Time, Patterson stealthily parked his car at the end of the Closs' driveway. Clad in a black coat and ski mask, he advanced toward the front door, shotgun in hand. James Closs, 56, confronted Patterson through a glass pane in the door, mistaking him for law enforcement and demanding to see a badge. Instead of identification, Patterson yelled a demand and fired his shotgun, tragically ending James' life.

The terror escalated as Patterson barged into the house, methodically checking each room with a chilling goal: leave no witnesses. He discovered the bathroom door locked, behind which Denise Closs, 46, was desperately comforting a terrified Jayme. The sound of the shotgun blasting through the door must have been deafening. At exactly 12:53 a.m., in the midst of this horror, Denise managed to make a 911 call, a call that would be her last act of protection for her daughter.

The 911 operator, though receiving no direct response from Denise, could hear the disturbing sounds of the ongoing assault. The line went dead shortly after, and subsequent attempts to call back reached only Denise's voicemail. Patterson then brutally ended Denise's life before abducting Jayme, binding her and placing her in his car trunk.

The police response was swift, arriving just four minutes after the 911 call. Unbeknownst to them, Patterson was mere seconds ahead, evading capture by the narrowest of margins as deputies rushed to the scene. Neighbors reported hearing the gunshots but, in a rural area accustomed to hunting, thought little of it at the time.

Patterson took Jayme to a remote cabin, imposing further horrors upon her. He forced her into different clothes and made her hide under his mattress, creating a prison from which there was no escape. This chilling confinement marked the beginning of 88 days of captivity for Jayme.

In a bizarre twist, less than two weeks into Jayme's abduction, an unrelated burglar broke into the Closs home, stealing items including Jayme's clothing. The man was apprehended, but he was not linked to the abduction or the murders.

In the bleak winter of 2019, the story of Jayme Closs' captivity under Jake Patterson took a dramatic turn, one marked by courage and a desperate bid for freedom. Patterson, under the delusion that fear had completely subdued Jayme, arrogantly believed she would never attempt an escape. He felt so secure in this belief that he never felt the need to fortify the cabin with extra locks or restraints. Their living arrangement was disturbingly intimate and controlled, with both sleeping on the same bed in the cramped, secluded cabin.

Patterson's control over Jayme extended to the rare occasions he allowed her outside. These brief walks on the cabin's lawn were always preceded by meticulous checks for any potential witnesses. But on January 10, 2019, a window of opportunity cracked open for Jayme. Patterson informed her he would be away for a few hours, following his routine of confining her under his bed, barricading her with various items.

Seizing this rare moment, Jayme mustered all her courage and strength. As soon as Patterson's car disappeared from view, she pushed aside the objects trapping her and fled into the frigid Wisconsin winter, clad only in a light shirt, leggings, and a pair of Patterson's oversized sneakers. Her escape was a race against time and elements.

Fate intervened when Jayme encountered Jeanne Nutter, a local woman walking her dog. The recognition was instant; Nutter knew Jayme from the relentless news coverage. Without hesitation, Nutter led Jayme to the nearest neighbor's house, a safe haven where they could call the police. The neighbors were struck by Jayme's appearance — calm yet dazed, quiet yet visibly shocked, and surprised that they recognized her.

The police response was swift and efficient, arriving around 4:45 p.m. to whisk Jayme to safety. The description she provided of Patterson and his vehicle was crucial. Remarkably, as deputies canvassed the area, they spotted Patterson's car. The arrest was almost cinematic: upon being stopped, Patterson stepped out and surrendered, admitting to his heinous crimes.

Jayme's rescue was a moment of profound relief. She was admitted to a hospital under guard, a necessary precaution given the gravity of her ordeal. In a heartwarming turn of events, the following morning, she was released into the loving care of her aunt, Jennifer Smith.

The saga of Jayme Closs's abduction and escape captured the attention of the nation, and in an act of solidarity and recognition, Hormel Foods — the parent company of Jennie-O, where Jayme's parents were employed — announced a reward of $25,000. This reward was not for information leading to her rescue, but rather awarded directly to Jayme for her bravery and resilience in rescuing herself. This gesture acknowledged the extraordinary courage of a young girl who faced unimaginable horrors and emerged with her spirit unbroken.

The life of Jake Patterson, prior to the heinous acts that would make headlines nationwide, was seemingly unremarkable but marked by personal disruptions and missed connections. His parents divorced in 2007, a potentially tumultuous event in any young person's life. Patterson's high school years at Northwood High School in Minong, Wisconsin, culminated in his graduation in 2015. His post-high school journey briefly led him to enlist in the U.S. Marine Corps, a path that ended abruptly with a discharge just one month later at MCRD San Diego. This early termination of service hinted at underlying issues that would later manifest in devastating ways.

Investigators delving into the abduction of Jayme Closs and the murder of her parents found no prior connection between Patterson and the Closs family. There was no evidence of social media contact, nor did the Closs relatives recognize Patterson's name. Patterson himself chillingly recounted to authorities that he first noticed Jayme Closs in September, seeing her alight from a school bus. It was a moment that would disastrously alter many lives; Patterson claimed he instantly decided to abduct her.

Patterson's grandfather painted a picture of a shy, withdrawn individual, far removed from the brutality of his actions. According to him, Patterson was quiet, often shying away from crowds, and more inclined towards computer games than social interactions. This portrayal starkly contrasts with the horrific acts Patterson would later commit, leaving his family utterly heartbroken and bewildered.

In the legal aftermath of his arrest, Patterson's confession to the police was straightforward. He admitted to kidnapping Jayme Closs and killing her parents. With no prior criminal record in Wisconsin, his sudden emergence as a perpetrator of such violent crimes was shocking. He faced charges of two counts of first-degree intentional homicide, kidnapping, and armed burglary. His bail was set at an imposing $5 million.

During the court proceedings, Patterson pleaded guilty to the homicide and kidnapping charges, resulting in the dismissal of the armed burglary count. He was ultimately sentenced to two consecutive life sentences without the possibility of parole for the murders, plus an additional 40 years for the kidnapping. Douglas County authorities chose not to pursue charges related to Jayme's captivity, focusing instead on securing a life sentence without parole.

While incarcerated, Patterson's communications revealed a conflicted and disturbed individual. In a letter to a reporter, he expressed remorse for his impulsive actions, a stark contradiction to the detailed planning described by police. He claimed his guilty plea was intended to spare Jayme and her family further trauma. In a phone call with a reporter, he described a disturbingly mundane captivity, filled with watching TV, playing board games, and cooking.

The aftermath of his sentencing brought little solace to those affected. His father, bearing a note of apology intended for Jayme, reflected the family's struggle to come to terms with Patterson's actions. As Patterson was officially registered as a sex offender and faced a transfer to an out-of-state prison, his brief and violent encounter with another inmate in New Mexico further underscored the turbulent and destructive path his life had taken.

Dorothy Scott

orothy Jane Scott, the cherished only child of Jacob and Vera Scott from Anaheim, California, entered the world on April 23, 1948. Amidst the cultural revolution of the mid-1960s, Dorothy, even as she celebrated her 18th birthday, remained steadfast in her conservative ethos. This was a time when many of her peers were passionately embracing the winds of change, advocating for women's rights, and exploring new, liberated lifestyles. Yet, Dorothy's path seemed quietly different, marked by a deep-seated conservatism.

Her life took a significant turn when she entered into a relationship with Dennis Terry. The couple welcomed their son, Sean, in 1976, infusing Dorothy's life with new responsibilities and joys. However, the serenity of this new family was short-lived. Following a breakdown in their relationship, Dennis Terry relocated to Fairgrove, Missouri, leaving Dorothy to navigate the complexities of single motherhood.

In an effort to provide for herself and Sean, Dorothy accepted secretarial positions in two shops in Anaheim, owned by the same entrepreneur. Intriguingly, one of these shops, the Swingers Psych Shop, co-founded by her father, epitomized the spirit of the era with its Woodstock flair. It was a haven for those seeking love beads, lava lamps, and incense. The other shop, Custom John's Head Shop, provided a contrast, yet both were conveniently located near her parents' home. This proximity allowed Dorothy to juggle her duties as a single mother with the demands of her job, as her parents often cared for

Sean while she worked.

People in Dorothy's life had nothing but admiration for her. They saw her as a doting mother, a loyal friend, and a woman deeply committed to her Christian faith. Unlike many of her contemporaries, she steered clear of the party scene, abstaining from alcohol and drugs. Instead, she devoted her free time to Sean and attended church regularly. Her colleagues at work knew her as reliable and organized, someone who brought a sense of calm and order to the workplace.

From the outside, Dorothy's life appeared unremarkable, almost mundane. Her friends would jokingly describe it as "boring with a capital B." If one were to paint her life, it would be in soft, unobtrusive colors – nothing too bright or too bold. But in May 1980, this tranquil canvas of Dorothy's life was suddenly overshadowed by ominous shades. She began receiving unsettling and bizarre phone calls, marking the onset of a new chapter in her life.

The early months of 1980 unfolded a sinister chapter in Dorothy Jane Scott's life, one filled with an unsettling blend of affection and malice. An unidentified man began to plague her with phone calls that oscillated between declarations of love and spine-chilling threats. Dorothy recognized the timbre of his voice, yet she couldn't pinpoint exactly who he was. Perhaps he was just an acquaintance she had casually interacted with, now turned into a shadowy figure haunting her life.

At times, this enigmatic caller would profess his love for Dorothy in a disturbingly obsessive manner. However, it was a particular moment, a call laced with a harrowing promise of violence, that revealed the true nature of this interaction. It became increasingly evident that this man was not just a random caller; he was a stalker, deeply obsessed with Dorothy, possessing an unnerving awareness of her daily activities, her attire, and her companions. It was as if he was shadowing her every move, possessing insights that only someone in close proximity could have.

Dorothy's mother, Vera, recalled a particularly chilling incident. One day, the caller instructed Dorothy to go outside, claiming he had left something for her. With a growing sense of dread, Dorothy complied, only to discover a solitary dead rose lying ominously on her car's windshield. In another terrifying call, the stalker's intentions were laid bare in a threat so graphic and menacing that it shook Dorothy to her core: he vowed to capture her and dismember her, ensuring that no one would ever find her remains.

These calls instilled a pervasive sense of fear in Dorothy, casting a shadow over her every moment, whether at home or work. The knowledge that an unseen, malevolent observer was tracking her stirred a deep unease in her heart. Confronted with the danger that lurked, Dorothy contemplated acquiring a gun for protection. However, the presence of her young son, Sean, in the house weighed heavily on her mind. She feared the potential harm a firearm could pose to the four-year-old.

Determined to find a way to defend herself, Dorothy chose a different path. She began taking karate lessons, arming herself with the skills she might need to protect herself and her son. These lessons were not just about physical defense; they were a testament to her resilience and her refusal to be rendered powerless in the face of a hidden, ominous threat.

As the fateful month of May in 1980 drew to a close, a seemingly routine day unfolded for 32-year-old Dorothy Jane Scott. It was Wednesday, May 28th, and Dorothy began her day as usual, dropping off her son Sean at her parents' house in Anaheim. She mentioned to them about a staff meeting scheduled for 9:00 PM at her workplace, Swinger's Psych Shop, and informed them she would be late in picking up Sean.

Dorothy then proceeded to her job, expecting a day like any other. However, during the meeting, she noticed something amiss with her colleague, Conrad Bostron. He appeared visibly unwell, suffering from pain and showing alarming signs of red swelling on his arm. Recognizing the seriousness of his condition, Dorothy, ever the empathetic and caring individual, offered to drive Conrad to the hospital. Accompanying them was another colleague, Pam Head.

In an era before the widespread use of cell phones, Dorothy needed to inform her parents about the change in her plans. She stopped by their house to update them about taking Conrad to the hospital, unsure of when she would return to pick up Sean. After a quick check on her son, Dorothy switched her black scarf for a red one and set off in her white 1973 Toyota station wagon to the UC Irvine Medical Center.

At the hospital, it was discovered that Conrad had been bitten by a black widow spider, leading to an infected bite. He received treatment from a doctor, who then prescribed medication. While Conrad was being treated, Dorothy and Pam waited in the ER, passing time by watching TV and browsing through magazines.

It was around 11 PM when Conrad was finally discharged. The three colleagues momentarily split up – Conrad and Pam went to the pharmacy to fill his prescription, while Dorothy offered to bring her car to the hospital entrance. This gesture was to spare Conrad any unnecessary exertion. Before heading to the parking lot, Dorothy excused herself to use the restroom.

Little did anyone know, this ordinary gesture would mark a significant and tragic turning point. The moment Dorothy stepped away to retrieve her car, she vanished into the night. The restroom visit was the last confirmed sighting of Dorothy Scott alive. Her disappearance under such mundane circumstances only added to the mystery and dread that had been building around her life.

The unsettling evening unfolded further as Conrad and Pam, clutching the newly obtained medication, stood expectantly at the hospital entrance. They were waiting for Dorothy to return with her car, but there was no sign of her. Concerned, they ventured towards the parking area where the car had been originally parked. As they walked, a startling sight greeted them – Dorothy's white 1973 Toyota station wagon hurtled towards them. The headlights were ablaze, making it impossible to see who was behind the wheel. To their dismay, the car didn't slow down or stop to pick them up. Instead, it swiftly turned onto the road and sped away into the night.

Puzzled and worried, Conrad and Pam initially thought that perhaps Dorothy had rushed off due to an emergency involving her son. They lingered at the hospital, clinging to the hope that Dorothy would soon return. But as time passed and there was still no sign of her, they felt a growing sense of unease. They reached out to the hospital security, only to be reassured that there was no cause for concern since Dorothy was an adult. Yet, the hours continued to tick by without any word from Dorothy, compelling her colleagues to make a distressing call to her parents, Vera and Jacob, to inquire if Dorothy had picked up Sean. The Scotts, too, had not heard from their daughter, deepening the mystery and concern.

As dawn approached on May 29th, around 4:30 AM, a significant yet disturbing discovery was made. Dorothy's car was found abandoned in Santa Ana, approximately 10 miles from the UC Irvine Medical Center. The car was empty, and there was no sign of Dorothy or any potential abductor. Worse still, the vehicle had been set on fire in an alleyway, a sinister act that only added to the horror of the situation. The police, who had initially not expressed much concern, were now fully alerted to the gravity of the case.

The Scott family was plunged into an abyss of agony and uncertainty, haunted by the baffling circumstances of Dorothy's disappearance. Their ordeal was exacerbated by the chilling continuation of phone calls from the anonymous stalker, even after Dorothy had vanished. About a week following her disappearance, Vera Scott, alone at home, received a call. The male voice on the other end inquired if she was related to Dorothy. When Vera affirmed, the voice chillingly claimed, "I've got her," before abruptly hanging up.

This call provided the first tangible link to Dorothy's disappearance, but pursuing it led nowhere, leaving the authorities and the Scott family no closer to unraveling the mystery of what had happened to Dorothy.

In a state of growing desperation and with little progress in the investigation, Dorothy's parents made a heart-wrenching decision. Despite warnings from the authorities to avoid the media to prevent potentially hindering the investigation, the Scotts could no longer bear the weight of silence. One week of fruitless waiting was intolerable. Overwhelmed with grief and the need for answers, Jacob and Vera reached out to the Orange County Register, sharing the harrowing tale of their daughter's mysterious disappearance in a desperate bid for any information that might lead to finding her.

The publication of Dorothy Jane Scott's mysterious disappearance in the local newspaper added a new, chilling dimension to the case. On June 12, 1980, the managing editor of the paper, Pat Riley, received a haunting phone call from an unidentified man. His words were ominous: "I killed her. I killed Dorothy Scott. She was my love, I caught her cheating with another man. She denied having someone else. I killed her."

The caller's intimate knowledge of the events on that fateful night was deeply unsettling. He accurately described that Dorothy had changed from a black scarf to a red one before leaving for the hospital with Conrad Bostron, who needed treatment for a spider bite. Furthermore, he claimed that Dorothy had called him from the hospital on the night she disappeared. This assertion, however, was disputed by Pam Head, who insisted she was with Dorothy the entire time at the hospital. The two had only briefly separated when Dorothy went to retrieve her car, while Pam accompanied Conrad to the pharmacy.

This mysterious man, who seemed to be aware of such specific details of that night, left everyone baffled. Who was he, and how did he know so much?

The call to Mr. Riley was deeply troubling for Dorothy's parents and friends.

Jacob Scott, her father, stated that Dorothy had no boyfriend and seldom went on dates due to her busy life juggling two jobs and caring for her son, Sean.

As the months and years passed, with the investigation yielding no definitive outcome, the anonymous caller continued to torment Dorothy's parents. He seemed to know the routines of Jacob and Vera Scott well, making his calls a dreaded Wednesday afternoon routine for four years, particularly targeting Vera when she was home alone. He would mentally torment Mrs. Scott with claims of either having Dorothy or having killed her.

The ominous calls finally ceased in April 1984, nearly four years after Dorothy's disappearance. The last call was made in the evening and answered by Jacob for the first time. Was the caller deterred by the possibility of being recognized by Jacob, or was he startled to hear a different voice? Despite these disturbing calls, the Scotts never changed their phone number, holding onto the slim hope that their daughter's abductor might allow them to speak with her.

In August 1984, the Scott family received a distressing call from the authorities. Human and dog bones had been discovered, and there was a possibility they belonged to Dorothy.

On the morning of August 6, 1984, construction company foreman Jesse Loza made a grim discovery in northeast Anaheim. Just after jesting with his crew to be wary of dead bodies as they prepared to lay pipes for telephone lines, he found a partially charred adult human skeleton, alongside the remains of a dog, near Eucalyptus Drive. Initially, the Orange County Deputy Coroner, Richard Rodriguez, speculated that the person may have been hiking with their dog when they met with an unfortunate incident. The bones, burned likely due to a brush fire that swept through the area in 1982, were estimated to have been there for over two years. Among the remains were a complete skull, two femurs, a pelvis, and an arm – all bleached white from sun exposure. Fortunately, the skull was intact and contained a full set of teeth with fillings.

Judy Suchey, an anthropologist from Cal State Fullerton, was brought in to help determine the age and sex of the remains and to compare the teeth against the missing person's database. Alongside the human remains, a turquoise ring and a watch that had stopped at 12:30 AM on May 29th were discovered, coinciding with the approximate time Dorothy's vehicle was seen speeding away from the hospital. On August 14th, the remains were identified as Dorothy's through dental records.

However, even after confirming that the remains belonged to Dorothy, the cause of her death remained undetermined. Just two days after the identification, the sinister caller made another call to the Scott household, coldly inquiring, "Is Dorothy there?" Despite efforts by the police to tap the phone and trace the caller, he never stayed on the line long enough to be located.

Dorothy was laid to rest on August 22nd, with her case unresolved and still shrouded in mystery.

Regrettably, no one was ever officially named a suspect, and no arrests were made in connection to Dorothy's case. Dennis Terry, Sean's father, was investigated but ruled out as a suspect since he was in Missouri at the time of Dorothy's disappearance. In a 2017 blog interview, Sean mentioned a coworker of his mother's named Mike Butler, whom he suspected of being involved. Butler, allegedly part of an occult group and holding unconventional religious beliefs, was reportedly fixated on Dorothy and knew her through his sister. Despite law enforcement's interest in him, there was never sufficient evidence to arrest or charge him.

The case of Dorothy Jane Scott remains an enduring mystery, a story that is as heartbreaking

as it is unresolved, leaving a haunting legacy of questions that may never be answered.

Roberta Ferguson

oberta Marie Ferguson's journey through life is a richly woven narrative, filled with cultural diversity, personal achievements, and adversities. She came into the world on November 19, 1968, in the vast expanses of Canada, as the youngest of nine siblings in a lively household. Her parents, Aaron E. and Mary Ferguson, nurtured a deep connection to their heritage, blending elements from First Nations and European settler cultures, notably the Dunvegan Beaver Band. This fusion of cultures deeply influenced Roberta, shaping her perspective and values.

Growing up in Grimshaw, a charming town in Northern Alberta celebrated for its tight-knit community and tranquil settings, Roberta's artistic side flourished. She found joy and expression in drawing and dancing, which allowed her to encapsulate the essence of her surroundings and cultural background. Known for her love of reading and her flair for humor, Roberta was both reflective and playful, often immersing herself in a world filled with imagination and comedy.

Under the guidance of her mother, Mary, a figure of strength and resilience, Roberta and her siblings were raised to be bold and self-assured. Despite facing racial discrimination due to their darker skin, Mary's teachings empowered her children to confront such challenges with courage. This lesson was especially significant for Roberta, who shared a deep connection with her mother.

A pivotal moment in Roberta's life occurred at the age of 14 when her mother, Mary, passed away from lupus, leaving a profound gap in her life. This loss was intensified by Roberta's own health struggles; she was born with a heart defect, which she managed with medication and determination. The passing of her mother represented a significant shift in Roberta's path, altering her life in unexpected ways.

As time progressed, Roberta's life became a journey of exploration and personal development. She found a comforting haven living with her sisters Carol and Marilyn in Edmonton, where she experienced a sense of belonging and support. She also spent enlightening summers with another sister in Surrey, dedicating this time to contemplation and future planning. During these years, Roberta nurtured ambitions of finishing high school and envisioned a life brimming with love and companionship. She often expressed her desires for marriage to her boyfriend.

The summer of 1988 marked a crucial period in Roberta's journey. That August, at 19, she went on a camping trip to Sunnyside Campground at Cultus Lake in British Columbia. The trip was more than a leisurely outing; it was a celebration with friends and family, including her niece, to commemorate her completion of a work-study program. Yet, despite this milestone, Roberta was introspective and somewhat reserved. Confronting health challenges and the emotional intricacies of her early twenties, she approached this critical time with a mix of uncertainty and optimism.

As dusk settled over the serene Cultus Lake, a deep yearning for home's comfort overcame Roberta. She expressed to her friends her wish to return home, choosing to take the bus. She left the campground around 8 p.m., unknowingly leaving the final visible footprint of her presence there.

The following morning, a profound unease hung over the Ferguson family. Known for her thoughtful nature and regular contact with her family, Roberta's sudden and unusual disappearance was deeply worrying. Her unexplained absence and failure to communicate her whereabouts were out of character, sparking immediate concern among her loved ones.

In their search for clarity, the Ferguson family reached out to law enforcement, but their initial efforts were met with a discouraging reply. Misinformed that it was premature to file a missing person report, they faced an unnecessary delay in the search. Contrary to this advice, Canadian law doesn't require a waiting period to report someone missing, a critical detail that was overlooked in Roberta's case. This misstep resulted in valuable time being lost, time that could have been crucial in finding her.

Fueled by determination and urgency, the Fergusons took proactive steps. They initiated a grassroots movement, creating and disseminating missing person flyers extensively, and even drove to Cultus Lake themselves, tirelessly searching for any sign of Roberta. Their efforts were a powerful display of familial solidarity and unwavering hope in locating her.

The police eventually intensified their efforts in the search, but the initial delay cast a pall over the investigation. The earliest moments following someone's disappearance are critical in gathering leads, and in Roberta's situation, this vital window had sadly passed without any significant breakthroughs.

Roberta's disappearance remained an unresolved enigma, with no definitive evidence or clues about her fate. Speculation arose, including the possibility that she might have intentionally started a new life elsewhere. Yet, this conjecture seemed incongruent with the known aspects of her life: her recent academic achievements, future plans with her partner, and her health issues. These elements suggested a young woman deeply connected to her current life, rendering the theory of her willingly starting over implausible.

Roberta was recognized by those close to her as a person of integrity, not given to reckless behavior with alcohol or drugs. She stayed away from party scenes and had no history of running away from home, presenting an image of a young woman accustomed to a stable and routine lifestyle.

The hypothesis of Roberta being abducted by an unknown individual is a prevalent theory, though it remains speculative without solid proof. This theory, and others, cause continual worry and conjecture for the Ferguson family, especially concerning the events preceding her disappearance. A notable issue is her friends' decision to let Roberta travel alone to the bus station, particularly considering her health condition at that time. It's argued that a more considerate action would have been to accompany her, ensuring her safety.

Another angle explored was the possibility that Roberta might have hitchhiked to the station, though it's unclear if she ever reached her destination. Subsequent to her leaving, there was a sighting of someone resembling Roberta engaging in conversation with a man in a red sports car at Vedder Mountain Road and Cultus Lake Road. The man, described as of average height with blond or light brown hair and a distinct jawline, remains unidentified, adding to the case's complexity.

The police have entertained the notion of foul play in Roberta's disappearance, investigating potential links to known criminals. One suspect was serial killer Robert Pickton, the notorious "Pig Farm Killer". Although Pickton typically targeted victims with a different profile than Roberta, the extensive nature of his crimes brought him into question. Yet, DNA samples from the Ferguson family did not correspond with any remains found on Pickton's farm.

Terry Arnold, a convicted murderer who once claimed to be the last person to see Roberta, was also scrutinized. His possession of a red hatchback at the time of her disappearance raised suspicions. Arnold, who died in 2005, left a note denying any involvement in Roberta's case and the crimes for which he was convicted. Despite this, the Fergusons suspect his involvement, but the full truth behind his alleged confession remains elusive.

When she disappeared, Roberta was described as 5 feet 5 inches tall, around 115 to 120 pounds, with long, curly dark brown or black hair, brown eyes, and often wearing glasses. Her last known outfit included octagon glasses, a blue-black tank top, knee-rolled black stretchy pants, white sneakers with dirt marks, and an army green backpack.

Roberta's case is one of many involving Indigenous women that has sadly lacked proper attention. A 2014 RCMP report categorized her case among 225 unsolved disappearances and murders of Indigenous women. Her sisters actively campaign for more comprehensive investigations into these cases, underscoring the urgent need for systemic changes in addressing such disappearances.

Audrey Groat

Born to Carl and Laura, Audrey was the second child to grace the family, a prelude to three more sisters and two brothers who would soon fill their home with an assortment of voices and laughter.

Audrey, with her dark hair and bright eyes, was a gentle presence, often described as soft-spoken, yet her laugh had the infectious power to light up a room. Her early years were spent in a modest blue-collar environment; her father worked diligently at Shoreline Washed Sand, a commercial sand plant, and was a dedicated member of the Teamsters Union.

From her early days, Audrey exhibited a unique blend of characteristics. She was strong-willed and fiercely independent, known for her outspokenness and a personality that friends likened to a combination of 'silk and sandpaper'. This blend of softness and strength became her signature trait, making her stand out in her small hometown of Killingworth, a quaint town in Middlesex County with less than a thousand residents at the time.

Despite the abundance of records about her family, details about Audrey's youth are sparse, like whispers lost in the winds of time. It wasn't until a spring day in 1972 that Audrey stepped out of the shadows of obscurity. By then, she had traveled 200 miles north to Barre, Vermont. On the eve of her 20th birthday, Audrey married James Victor Coate, a union marked by a simple ceremony officiated by the city clerk.

Audrey's journey into motherhood began in April 1973 with the birth of her first daughter. The family, then living in Montpelier, Vermont, faced their fair share of challenges. James, a self-employed painter, and Audrey, ever determined, juggled work and family life. Audrey was the kind of person who would take on multiple jobs if needed, never one to shy away from hard work or life's pressures.

The Groat family grew over the years, welcoming five more daughters. However, not all was serene in Audrey's life. The late 1970s saw her parents' marriage dissolve, and her own marriage to James began to falter. The 1980s brought more trials; as she and James prepared to separate, Audrey faced the heartache of her father's passing. Nevertheless, she remained a pillar of strength, taking on the role of a single mother to her six daughters, a challenge she met with her characteristic resilience.

After her divorce, life continued to test Audrey's fortitude. She moved her family to South Ryegate, then to Northfield, Vermont. In the late 1980s, a conversation with her daughters sparked a bold new venture: building their own home on a piece of land off Hallstrom Road. Together, they built a house that, despite lacking modern amenities like running water and electricity for several months, stood as a testament to their collective strength and unity.

Audrey's life took another twist when she met Patrick Jarvis, a colleague from Community Products in Montpelier. While their relationship's nature remains unclear, they shared a close bond, spending time with Audrey's family and working on the house together.

However, the early 1990s brought financial struggles for Audrey. A layoff from her job and the challenge of supporting her family tested her resilience once again. Despite these hardships, Audrey remained fiercely independent, reluctantly accepting government assistance only when necessary to provide for her daughters.

On the serene morning of Saturday, August 21st, Audrey Groat embarked on her usual weekend routine with a distinctive zest. She found solace in the outdoor haven of her property, immersing herself in nature while working on a stone wall and tending to the landscape. Audrey relished these moments, often kicking off her shoes to connect with the earth beneath her feet, a simple pleasure that brought her immense joy.

However, this particular Saturday held different plans for Audrey, plans that have since become a focal point of debate and intrigue. She was scheduled to meet with Patrick Jarvis, a detail that sparked a disagreement with her daughter Karina. Despite Karina's fervent desire to accompany her mother, Audrey, steadfast in her decision, gently refused. The exchange ended with Karina, then only 13, setting a playful yet earnest deadline for her mother's return - 6:30 pm. Little did they know, this would be a time Audrey would never meet.

The afternoon unfolded with Audrey leaving to drop another daughter at a friend's house in Middlesex, a moment that would later be remembered as the last confirmed sighting of her. Accompanied by Jarvis in his beige Ford Escort, she embraced her daughter, her maternal warmth evident in her parting words and assurances of returning the next morning.

As the day transitioned into night, Karina watched the clock tick past the agreed time. Initially, she didn't worry; Audrey was known for her punctuality, but occasional lateness wasn't unheard of. However, as the evening deepened into night with no sign of her mother, Karina's concern escalated. Repeated calls to Jarvis's apartment yielded no answers, only increasing her anxiety.

By 1 am, the roommate's annoyance was palpable, yet Karina's worry turned into a foreboding sense of dread. When morning arrived without a word from Audrey, Karina's initial annoyance transformed into profound worry. Meanwhile, the friends caring for Audrey's youngest daughter also began to sense that something was amiss. It was completely out of character for

Audrey to miss a pickup without any communication.

As the Northfield Police Department initiated their investigation, they pieced together Audrey's intended plans for the day. Her truck, a red and silver Chevy S10, was found at a park and ride, prompting theories about her whereabouts. Perhaps she had encountered trouble or taken an unexpected detour. The lack of any signs of a struggle or disturbance around her truck only deepened the mystery.

As the investigation progressed, police and the community grappled with the growing uncertainty. Flyers began to circulate, a tangible symbol of the community's concern and the urgent need to find Audrey. This grassroots effort eventually prompted the police to issue a public statement, elevating Audrey's disappearance from a simple missing person case to a mysterious and concerning situation.

Chief Michael O'Neal expressed the perplexing nature of the case, highlighting the oddity of Audrey's vanishing without a trace, without any indication of her intentions. As the investigation continued, everyone involved clung to the hope of finding answers, of unraveling the enigma that Audrey's disappearance had become.

Investigators, returning to the park and ride where Audrey's truck was discovered, conducted a thorough search of the area. It was during this meticulous sweep that they unearthed a critical clue: Audrey's purse, concealed in some bushes at the edge of the parking lot. This discovery, coupled with the fact that her keys were locked inside her truck, painted a concerning picture and spurred a decision to intensify the search.

The parking lot, abutting a sprawling wooded area, became the focal point of the investigation. Despite the thoroughness of the initial search, it yielded no tangible leads. The passing of time, combined with the discovery of Audrey's purse and the absence of any sightings, signaled to investigators that they were facing a case far more complex than a typical missing person's scenario. The Northfield Police Department, recognizing the magnitude of the situation and the limitations of their small force, called in the Vermont State Police for assistance.

On August 25th, a new phase of the investigation began as the state police took custody of Audrey's truck, transporting it to their barracks in Middlesex for a detailed examination. Plans were set in motion for a second, more expansive search of the park and ride's surrounding area. Despite these efforts, the subsequent search mirrored the first - no signs of Audrey were found.

By August 27th, the gravity of the situation was setting in. The state police, alongside 25 officers and local volunteers, conducted a painstaking three-hour search of the nearby woods. Yet again, the effort brought no new information about Audrey's whereabouts. The focus of the investigation shifted towards those in Audrey's life, with the Northfield Police re-interviewing individuals in the hope of uncovering a missed detail.

Chief O'Neal of the Northfield Police maintained a hopeful outlook, but Captain Kerry Sleeper of the State Police expressed a more somber perspective, acknowledging the increasing likelihood of foul play. The theory that Audrey might have taken time away on her own was still considered by some officers, but those who knew her, including her daughter Tanya, vehemently disagreed with this notion. Tanya's words to the reporters underscored her belief in her mother's commitment to her family.

Desperate for answers, Tanya reached out to Patrick Jarvis, the last known person to have seen Audrey. Jarvis claimed he had dropped Audrey off at her truck around 10 pm on Saturday and hadn't seen her since. This account led to the harrowing possibility that Audrey might have been attacked or even abducted from the parking lot, her purse discarded in the ensuing struggle.

Behind the scenes of the search for Audrey, a pressing concern arose: the care of her younger daughters. Tanya, only 18, took on the formidable task of caring for her sisters, a sudden and overwhelming responsibility that thrust her into adulthood.

Patrick Jarvis, the central figure in Audrey's last known movements, became a person of significant interest to the police. His account of the night painted a picture of a casual evening ending with him watching Audrey drive away in her truck. However, the police found inconsistencies and peculiarities in his story. As they delved deeper, they uncovered disturbing allegations against Jarvis, unrelated to Audrey's disappearance but equally alarming.

A wiretap on Jarvis's phone, authorized on August 31st, quickly led to his arrest on September 1st for aggravated sexual assault of a juvenile, based on accusations from a young relative of Audrey's. This arrest sparked a series of searches in areas Jarvis claimed to have visited the night Audrey vanished, including the Lamoille River and a remote campsite in Middlesex.

Sergeant Ross of the State Police articulated the police's heightened interest in Jarvis's whereabouts and activities. Concurrently, investigators began probing into whether anyone close to Audrey was aware of Jarvis's criminal history, which included a variety of offenses dating back to 1973.

As the investigation deepened, the focus shifted significantly toward Patrick Jarvis, particularly his criminal history outside Vermont. In South Carolina, Jarvis had a troubling past: In 1990, he pled guilty to lewd and lascivious acts with a minor under the age of 14, receiving a suspended sentence and probation. His violation of this probation led to his extradition back to South Carolina, where he served around 30 months. Friends of Audrey, speaking to the Burlington Free Press, expressed doubts that she knew about this aspect of Jarvis's past. However, police files later revealed that at least Angela, Audrey's eldest daughter, believed her mother was aware. Furthermore, sworn affidavits suggested Audrey had explicitly warned her daughters never to be alone with Jarvis, though she refrained from explaining her reasons.

Jarvis's cooperation with the police waned significantly when they intensified their questioning about Audrey and proposed a polygraph test. Choosing to remain silent, he requested legal counsel. This development complicated the investigation, limiting the police's ability to interrogate him further about the events of August 21st. In light of this, authorities conducted a second search of the Lamoille River, covering every location Jarvis claimed to have visited on the night Audrey disappeared, but to no avail.

During his arraignment on September 2nd, Jarvis pled not guilty. Given his history and the severity of the charges, which could lead to a life sentence, the judge deemed him a flight risk and set bail at $25,000. During the arraignment, Washington County State's Attorney Terry Trono hinted at Jarvis's potential involvement in Audrey's disappearance, a sentiment that fueled public speculation.

Meanwhile, Audrey's family grew increasingly frustrated with the lack of communication from the investigators. Laura, Audrey's mother, and Angela found themselves in the dark regarding the progress of the investigation. Laura even drove up from Connecticut in search of answers, as her calls to the authorities went unanswered.

Behind the scenes, the investigation was actively unfolding. Police conducted searches at Jarvis's apartment and his mother's home in Middlesex. While the specifics of what they were searching for remained undisclosed, the presence of a state police crime lab van indicated a serious inquiry. Freshly overturned earth on the mother's property piqued the investigators' interest, adding another layer to the complex investigation.

Amidst this, Audrey's daughters faced a challenging situation. Tanya, initially planning to assume guardianship of her sisters, withdrew her request as two local families stepped in to help, with one seeking guardianship of one girl and another willing to take in two. The judge overseeing the case requested consent forms from their biological father in New York before making any decisions.

In late September, the Burlington Free Press acquired several police documents related to Audrey's disappearance. One affidavit, reportedly based on the statements of one of Audrey's children, revealed a disturbing account of Jarvis removing a shovel from a cellar hole and placing it in his car the day after Audrey vanished. This revelation was a crucial factor in the earlier search of the campsite and surrounding woods.

The investigation continued to uncover unsettling details. A search of Jarvis's apartment early in September resulted in the confiscation of various items. Subsequently, on September 11th, following a tip from an anonymous source, police executed a second search, seizing a green sleeping bag, poetry, and other undisclosed items suggesting a motive.

On October 19th, legal complexities forced a reduction in charges against Jarvis. The aggravated assault charges, partly based on his South Carolina conviction, were changed to four counts of assault due to a technicality in the legal classification of his previous offense. This led to a reduction in his bail from $25,000 to $5,000, despite the state attorney's efforts to maintain the original charge.

As the investigation into Audrey's disappearance continued, progress seemed to stagnate. Captain O'Neal described the situation as a "waiting game," with the hope that the upcoming hunting season might lead to the discovery of evidence in a remote area. In early November, officials announced a planned search of the Wrightsville Dam and Reservoir area in Middlesex, scheduled for November 6th, as they continued their relentless pursuit of answers.

The mysterious location at the heart of the investigation, Wrightsville Dam and Reservoir in Middlesex, held a grim fascination due to its connection to Patrick Jarvis. Known for its swimming area and boat launch, Jarvis often visited this site with Audrey and her children, and it was located less than two miles from the secluded campsite where he claimed to have spent the night with Audrey before her disappearance. This crucial detail led the New England Canine Search and Rescue Squad to conduct a thorough search of the reservoir and its surroundings, where several cadaver dogs detected the scent of human decomposition near its southern part. This discovery prompted plans for an underwater search in this specific area of the reservoir, known to be over thirty feet deep and covering submerged farmland.

As the weather began to shift, signaling the approach of harsher conditions, the urgency to conduct the search escalated. The reservoir's depth and the impending seasonal change meant that land searches would soon become more challenging, and water searches nearly impossible. Compounding this urgency was a tip suggesting that Audrey's body might be located in a significant body of water in the Middlesex area.

On November 9th, the search intensified as eight divers braved the frigid, 40-degree waters of the reservoir. Working in pairs and hindered by poor visibility, the divers relied on touch and guidance from ropes connected to boats on the surface. Despite their exhaustive efforts from 10:30 a.m. to 4:00 p.m., they found no evidence linked to Audrey. Although this result was disheartening, police acknowledged the difficulty of the search and did not rule out the possibility that Audrey could still be there. In the following weeks, several visitors to the reservoir reported a foul odor in the area that had been searched, adding to the mystery.

Meanwhile, the guardianship of Audrey's daughters was finally resolved in early December. A local soccer coach and his family welcomed Audrey's youngest daughter, while her friend and mechanic, Jim Lambert, and his wife Judy took in two of her other daughters. A fourth daughter chose to move to New York to live with her estranged father. However, the absence of proof of Audrey's death meant that her children were ineligible for social security benefits and government financial assistance, as they were living with non-blood relatives.

On December 7th, Patrick Jarvis accepted a plea deal, requiring him to undergo a polygraph test. The terms of the deal, which included confidentiality regarding the polygraph results, were shaped partly by the victim's unwillingness to testify and a psychiatric evaluation suggesting potential trauma from doing so. Jarvis pleaded guilty to one charge of lewd and lascivious conduct with a child, receiving a sentence of one to five years, with three years suspended. His time served since September would count towards this sentence, and upon release, he would be on probation, barred from contact with anyone under 16, and required to undergo counseling. As part of the deal, Jarvis admitted to the sexual acts on the child in court. The polygraph test, taken later that week, lasted three hours, though its results remained undisclosed.

The year 1993 closed with Jarvis in jail, Audrey still missing, and the investigation stalled by weather and lack of new leads. In February 1994, Gary and Judy Lambert sought legal help to prove Audrey's death and secure her children's death benefits, a situation that concerned police about potential interference with their investigation. As the area thawed in May, new searches were planned, including a July investigation of a discovery of human hair in Marshfield Pond, yet nothing conclusive linked to Audrey was found.

Police searched various locations, including a junkyard in Middlesex, but found no evidence. They began to suspect that Audrey never made it to her truck the night she vanished and might not have visited the mall. They theorized she confronted Jarvis about his assault against the child, leading to her disappearance. While Jarvis remained a person of interest, he was not the sole suspect. By the end of 1994, frustration and concern grew among Audrey's friends and family as time passed with no significant progress.

On December 20th, Jarvis was released after serving 15 months, remaining on probation for three years. Investigators expressed their frustration with the lack of a breakthrough in the case, emphasizing their commitment to due process and the necessity of concrete evidence for any arrest.

In April 1995, the Rutland Daily Herald delved into the perplexing case of Audrey Groat's disappearance, featuring insights from investigators, Audrey's daughters, the Lamberts, and attorney Gary McQueston. The story unearthed several new details about the night Audrey went missing and the subsequent efforts to find her.

The investigation into that fateful night in August 1993 revealed inconsistencies in Jarvis's statements. He had recounted a 40-mile journey to the mall with Audrey, a stop at Wendy's where his vivid memory of ordering chili contrasted sharply with his vague recollections of the routes taken. After their meal, Jarvis claimed they traveled back to Montpelier, stopped for beer and cigarettes, and then went to a tented area near Baldur Road in Middlesex. Here, Jarvis's account included drinking six beers each and engaging in sexual activity before supposedly dropping Audrey off at the park and ride. However, his story altered upon subsequent questioning, with one version stating he saw her still in her truck 30 minutes after dropping her off and another suggesting she might have needed an alternate ride home.

Audrey's daughter, in a sworn statement, recounted confronting Jarvis about her mother's whereabouts, to which he suggested Audrey had vanished after attempting to call someone. Jarvis's claim of then driving around Burlington and fishing until dawn raised further doubts, given the distance and alcohol consumption he reported.

Investigators expressed skepticism regarding Jarvis's account, doubting Audrey's presence at the mall or Wendy's that night. A receipt from the mall, time-uncertain, was found in Jarvis's apartment, but the item purchased — strawberry flavored motion lotion — was later linked to the sexual assault of his young victim. Police also believed Jarvis spent around two hours at the Baldur Road campsite.

Friends and family challenged Jarvis's portrayal of his relationship with Audrey, emphasizing her disinterest in a romantic or sexual relationship with him and her infrequent drinking, casting doubt on the plausibility of her consuming six beers in a tent.

Despite nearly a dozen searches, investigators found no trace of Audrey. Lieutenant O'Leary reflected on the challenges of the investigation, highlighting the need for a lucky break while maintaining their solid theories on the case.

Attorney Gary McQueston had twice tried to have Audrey officially declared deceased, but the lack of evidence hindered these efforts. In February 1996, he submitted a comprehensive report to the court, emphasizing the urgency for her children's sake. During a hearing, Jarvis, called to the stand, invoked his Fifth Amendment right against self-incrimination.

Six months later, in September, a superior court judge ordered a death certificate for Audrey, presuming her death and listing August 21, 1993, as her date of death. In October 1997, Audrey's daughters held a memorial service in Connecticut, placing a headstone with a message of love and remembrance.

Sergeant Mike Henry, recently taking over the case, attended a 2006 service held by Audrey's daughters at the park and ride. Angela, Audrey's eldest, expressed the torment of not knowing what happened to their mother.

In April 2009, 16 years after Audrey's disappearance, the Vermont State Police, the Montpelier Police, and the New England Canine Search team explored a previously unsearched wooded area near the park and ride, following a tip received in November 2008. Despite extensive efforts, nothing connected to Audrey was found.

Captain Edward Leto of the Vermont State Police remained confident that answers were out there, suggesting that there were individuals who knew the truth about what happened to Audrey Groat.

About the Author

Margaret Snead is a name that has become synonymous with the gripping and meticulous unraveling of some of the most complex and chilling true crime stories of our time. A seasoned journalist with a career spanning over two decades, Margaret's journey into the world of true crime writing began with her fascination for the intricacies of criminal psychology and the profound impact of crime on human lives and society.

Born and raised in Chicago, Illinois, Margaret's early exposure to the diverse urban landscape fueled her curiosity about the human condition and the darker corners of urban life. She pursued her passion for writing and story-telling at Northwestern University, where she earned a degree in Journalism. Her early career saw her working in various local newspapers, where she honed her skills in investigative journalism.

Margaret's transition to true crime writing was marked by her first book, a deep dive into a notorious serial crime case that had haunted her hometown for years. Her meticulous research, attention to detail, and compassionate narrative voice quickly earned her accolades and a dedicated following. Her approach to storytelling is unique in that she focuses not only on the crime itself but also on the psychological aspects of the criminal mind and the ripple effects of crime on victims, families, and communities.

Over the years, Margaret Snead has authored several best-selling true crime books, each meticulously researched and written with a blend of factual precision and compelling prose. Her work often involves years of research, including interviews with law enforcement, psychologists, witnesses, and, when possible, the criminals themselves. She is known for her ability to weave complex information into a narrative that is both informative and engrossing, making the dark world of crime accessible and understandable to her readers.

Aside from her writing, Margaret is a sought-after speaker at literary festivals and crime writing workshops, where she shares her insights into crime writing and investigative journalism. Her contributions to the genre have not only enlightened readers but have also brought attention to lesser-known cases and the importance of justice and closure for those affected.

Margaret Snead's dedication to uncovering the truth and telling the stories that need to be told has established her as a formidable figure in the world of true crime literature. Her books not only captivate readers but also contribute to a deeper understanding of the complexities and consequences of crime in modern society.